WRITE YOUR OWN

EGYPTIAN HIEROGLYPHS

Write Your Own Egyptian Hieroglyphs

Angela McDonald

University of California Press
Berkeley Los Angeles

University of California Press, one of the most distinguished university presses in the United States, enriches lives around the world by advancing scholarship in the humanities, social sciences, and natural sciences. Its activities are supported by the UC Press Foundation and by philanthropic contributions from individuals and institutions. For more information, visit www.ucpress.edu.
University of California Press

Berkeley and Los Angeles, California

First published by British Museum Press, a division of the British Museum Company Ltd
38 Russell Square, London WC1B 3QQ

Library of Congress Cataloging-in-Publication Data

McDonald, Angela.
Write your own Egyptian hieroglyphs / Angela McDonald.
p. cm.
Includes bibliographical references and index.
ISBN-13: 978-0-520-25235-6 (pbk. : alk. paper)
1. Egyptian language—Writing, Hieroglyphic. 2. Names, Egyptian. I. Title.

PJ1097.M35 2007
493'.111—dc22 2006051405

Designed and typeset by Chris Hulin, Oxford Book Projects
Manufactured in China

16 15 14 13 12 11 10 09 08 07
10 9 8 7 6 5 4 3 2 1

Angela McDonald pp 10, 14 top right, 30, 38, 45 bottom, 68.

The line drawings are by:

T.G.H. James p. 24.
Angela McDonald pp 53, 55 top, 56, 67, 72–3.
Richard Parkinson pp 28, 64.

Contents

Introduction – Be a Scribe!

'By day write with your fingers, recite by night.
Befriend the scroll and the palette – it's more fulfilling than wine!'

Papyrus Lansing. New Kingdom.

Palettes belonging to a painter (left) and a scribe (right). Both are made of wood with grooves for reed pens and ink wells for pigment. New Kingdom.

'Be a scribe!' is the cry that resounds in ancient Egyptian school-texts. These texts, like Papyrus Lansing quoted above, were copied out by boys learning the invaluable skill of writing. Apprentice scribes were promised status, prosperity and – most importantly – immortality through their ability to write. As one text warns – 'Man decays, his body withers to dust ... but writing causes him to be remembered.' Now you have a chance to join their ranks.

The aim of this book is to teach you how to write your own hieroglyphs. The emphasis is on understanding how the Egyptians composed names for the elements of their world and then showing you how to create names in hieroglyphs for yourself. There are practical guides throughout the book explaining how to use hieroglyphs to compose names for yourself, your friends, your pets, and even your house. There are step-by-step tips at the back of the book on how to draw some of the trickier signs.

There is no attempt to explain the grammar of ancient Egyptian as a language in detail, but chapter 1 presents some of the principles of the hieroglyphic script – how it was deciphered, how words are composed and how they are read – and shows you how to use the hieroglyphic 'alphabet'. Chapter 2 explores how people were given their names in Egyptian, as well as the terms given to family, friends and enemies – and shows you how to compose your own Egyptian name in hieroglyphs. Chapter 3 focuses on the names of the many gods of Egypt, from well-known state deities like Isis and Anubis to lesser known demons of darker character, and reveals how to create a divine persona for yourself (and even your house!). Chapter 4 examines the names the Egyptians gave to the wild and domestic animals they lived alongside, especially their pets, and shows you how to create an impressive Egyptian name for your own pet. It also explores how the Egyptians used animal hieroglyphs to represent human emotions. Chapter 5 is a collection of genuine Egyptian phrases – greetings, laments, and lots of insults – for you to use in your own compositions.

What's in a Name?

The name of a brave man is in his accomplishments; it will never perish in this land for all eternity.

The Biography of Ahmose, son of Ibana. New Kingdom.

Why concentrate on names? In ancient Egypt, the names of people, animals, places and things were much more than just labels; they held within them the spark of existence. Nothing could truly *be* until it was given a name, for a name constituted a solid identity and through that, a place in the world. Consequently, a great deal of meaning was invested in names so that they often reflected the essence of the person or thing that held them. By using this book and learning how to break down and understand Egyptian names for people, animals and the gods, you will see the ancient Egyptians' world through their eyes.

This simple stela was erected over the grave of a dwarf named *Neferet* ('Perfection'), sacrificed to continue his service to King Semerkhet. Early Dynastic Period.

The act of carving a name could make a person live forever; conversely, erasing that name could condemn him to oblivion. There are many testaments to the power of names in Egyptian history and mythology, but the brief, traumatic reign of the 'heretic' king Akhenaten (*c*.1353–1336 BC) is among the most poignant. *Akhenaten* ('The spirit of the Aten') famously abandoned the traditional name that would have made him the fourth *Amenhotep* ('Amun is content') of the glorious 18th Dynasty in order to reflect the twin passions that burned in him – his allegiance to his new god, the Aten, and his hatred of the god of his predecessors, Amun. He waged war on Amun, sending agents all over his empire to mutilate and hack out every image of him and every mention of

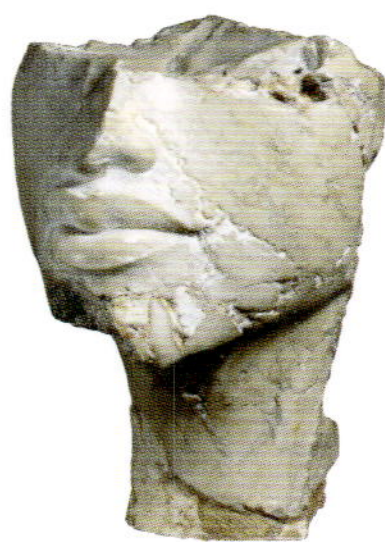
Deliberately damaged head of Akhenaten. New Kingdom.

his name, thereby erasing the god's existence. In an ironic twist of fate, Akhenaten suffered the same treatment at the hands of his successors who quickly returned to tradition. While Amun's names and images were re-carved to last, Akhenaten's own face and name, along with those of his family, were consigned to oblivion. If fragments (like the broken king's head from one of his many statues in the Aten's Great Temple at Amarna, left) survived, it was an accident of chance.

It was not just their meaning as words that gave names their power, but also the ways in which they were written. The hieroglyphs of the ancient Egyptian script constitute one of the most expressive writing systems in the world. They could convey both subtle and blatant nuances of meaning, most of which are inevitably lost when we try to translate them.

Throughout this book, you will explore the different levels of meaning the Egyptians invested in the names they chose for themselves and the elements of their world. You will see how the hieroglyphs with which names are written were used to affect their meaning. Just like an Egyptian scribe, you will be able to 'recite' your writings – every Egyptian word discussed in the various chapters is given in its original hieroglyphs, accompanied by an approximation of how to pronounce it (in italics), and a translation. So, go on – Be a scribe!

Statue of Pesshuper showing him in the pose of a scribe with a papyrus roll spread over his knees. He has a scribal palette sculpted on his left shoulder. Late Period.

Note about conventions
Throughout this book, hyphens are used to separate out more complex names and to indicate words that go together.

1 The Hieroglyphic Script

The Decipherment of Ancient Egyptian

For hundreds of years, some of the brightest scholars in the world struggled to 'crack the code' of Egyptian hieroglyphs. Most would-be decipherers followed guides such as the classical writer Horapollo, whose work *Hieroglyphica* was composed in the fifth century AD and rediscovered in the fifteenth. Most scholars were convinced that each hieroglyph communicated a mystical message. According to Horapollo, the 'night-owl' sign 𓅓 meant 'swift and sudden death' whereas it actually represents the sound of the letter 'm'. Even when Horapollo's readings of signs were close to the truth, they were still misleading for would-be translators; for example, his description of the *nefer* sign, 𓄤 , as 'a man's heart suspended from the windpipe' is correct. However, his translation of it as meaning 'the mouth of a good man' is not. As a word, *nefer* simply means 'perfect'.

Although hieroglyphs closely resemble objects from life they do not always represent them as words. Above: model of a man holding a hoe. Old Kingdom. Inset: hieroglyph in the shape of a hoe, standing for the sound *mer*. Middle Kingdom.

It was not until 1822 that a young French scholar named Jean-François Champollion finally realised that hieroglyphs (for the most part) were to be read as sounds and not ideas. Working with the trilingual inscription on the famous Rosetta Stone, Champollion was able to read the name of Ptolemy, and on that basis proved his theory. It was not long before he published an explanation of how the Egyptian script worked (*Précis du système hiéroglyphique des anciens égyptiens*, 1827–8), although his comprehensive grammar would only be published after his death (1836).

We are now in a position to read the vast assortment of texts the Egyptians left behind, both deliberately and by accident. This means we have at our disposal first-hand accounts of Egyptian science and maths, literature and love poems, ledgers and receipts, as well as the personal records of kings and noblemen. More than this, because the Egyptian script is so rich in self-explanation, we can gain an insight into how the Egyptians saw the world around them. The aim of this book is to share some of those insights and to let the modern reader see ancient Egypt through the eyes of its people.

Directions of Writing

Hieroglyphs can be written in many different directions – in horizontal lines from right to left and from left to right, downwards in columns, or curved around objects. The Egyptians loved symmetry, so often two sets of hieroglyphs will face each other as they do in the inscription on the left which wraps around a Ramesside Period column base in the ancient city of Memphis.

Even if you have no idea what an inscription says, you can easily figure out which direction to read it in. Look for an animate sign like a person, animal, or bird – animate signs always look towards the beginning of the inscription and so you read towards them. Thus in the inscription above, the two parts of the text start where the arrows branch out. One part of the text then reads from left to right (following the right arrow) while the other reads from right to left (following the left arrow). Notice that the signs that begin each inscription are 'interacting' with each other. The Egyptians believed that hieroglyphs in sacred spaces (like the walls and columns of tombs and temples, or the surfaces of stelae or obelisks) were alive and carved them with this in mind. Thus, the god sign to the right of the centre is literally offering a sign of courtesy (the hieroglyph for 'life': ☥ *ankh*) to the goose sign on the left.

In both parts of the column inscription above, signs have been placed not one after another, but often one under another. To the Egyptians' eyes, it looked 'neater' to tuck one short, broad sign under another rather than produce a line of single signs all of different shapes and sizes. Whether you are reading from left to right or vice versa, you always start with the sign on top and read downwards (see left).

The Order of Hieroglyphs

Occasionally the expected order of signs is changed. This is usually done for one of two reasons. Signs representing the name of a king or a god are usually put at the beginning of the words or phrases in which they occur: for example, the word for 'priest' (*hem netjer*) literally means 'servant of god'. It is written with the sign for 'servant' (*hem*) placed next to the sign for 'god' (*netjer*). Grammatically, the word 'servant' should come first, but the sign for 'god' is placed in front of it to show respect. Thus, *hem netjer* 'priest' is always written: . The technical term for this is *honorific transposition*.

The other reason for writing signs out of their proper order was purely aesthetic. It seemed neater to 'tuck' smaller signs into gaps left by larger signs, as in the example below:

This is known as *graphic transposition*.

The Sound of Ancient Egyptian

Like certain Semitic languages, the ancient Egyptian script only recorded consonants. There are equivalent sounds in Egyptian for most of the consonants in English (except 'c', 'v' and 'x' although these can be approximated). A list of these signs appears on page 19. At the same time, there are sounds in Egyptian that do not have equivalents in English: for example, there are four different types of 'h' sounds (see page 75). There are also four 'semi-consonants' which Egyptologists tend to pronounce as vowels:

is an '*i*' sound and is rather like our 'y'. It is technically a consonant (e.g. in words like 'yonder' and 'yellow'), but it behaves occasionally like a vowel (e.g. in 'by').

(right) is a '*w*' sound, but sometimes is closer to 'u'. It has an abbreviated form: .

Painted quail chick (*w*) hieroglyph. Middle Kingdom.

The last two semi-consonants are really supposed to be sounds made with the back of the throat which have no direct equivalent sound in English:

 is a 'glottal stop' - a sound made by opening your mouth and trying to close your throat at the same time. It is conventionally pronounced as an 'a'.

also represents a sound made in the back of the throat, but we tend to pronounce it as an 'e' or an 'a'.

Despite the presence of these semi-consonants, there are many words in Egyptian that are written with no vowel sounds at all. This is a problem when it comes to reading these words aloud because vowels are vital for sounding words out. How would you read this sentence without its vowels?

To cope with this problem, Egyptologists have worked out a system of vocalizing words written in hieroglyphs which simply fills in the many blanks left by the absence of vowels with an 'e' sound. Thus, the sign which represents the three consonants *n* + *f* + *r* is pronounced *nefer*.

Inevitably when it comes to pronunciation there are inconsistencies. Some Egyptologists call the sun-god Ra, while others call him Re. You will notice both spellings become part of names. Similarly, although the Theban god Amun's name should really be pronounced 'Imen', this is not usually done. You will usually find it appearing as 'Amun' and 'Amen' in names. Kings' names are usually the most subject to variations in writing: you will see writings like Ramses, Rameses, Ramesses, and so on, all naming the same king. It is confusing, but it is just something to get used to.

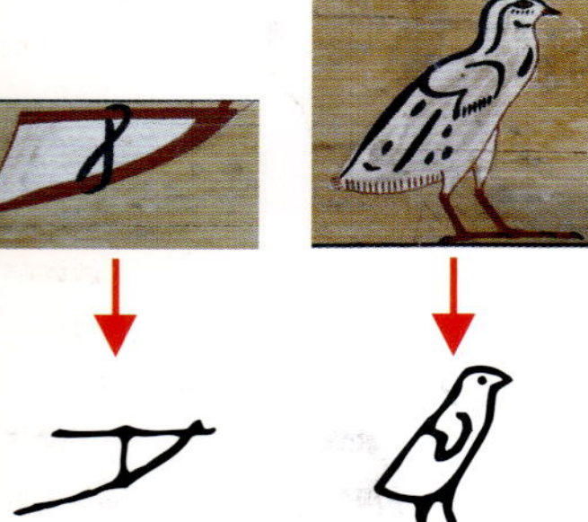

Types of Script

In this book the hieroglyphs are printed using a special Egyptian type font that shows each sign clearly and in a standardized way (see left). But on ancient Egyptian objects you may see writing in many different styles, and in various different scripts.

To the Egyptians, formal religious and historical inscriptions like those carved onto the walls of pyramids and temples demanded a kind of treatment different from legal documents and records of business transactions. Pyramid Texts and royal inscriptions were therefore carved in the most formal and ornate script – hieroglyphs – whereas administrative documents and personal texts like letters were written in hieratic, a quicker, more 'joined-up' version of the hieroglyphic script.

Both hieroglyphic and hieratic texts could be rendered in a variety of styles, which often depended on the materials a scribe was working with. If an inscription was to be written on a hard surface like granite, it was common for the signs to be carved in outline without much internal detail (see, for example, the Rosetta Stone below).

Hieroglyphs

Demotic

Greek

The text on the Rosetta Stone is written three times in different scripts – hieroglyphs at the top, demotic in the middle and Greek at the bottom – acknowledging the mixed Greek and Egyptian community of the time (196 BC). Demotic took over from hieratic as the script for less formal texts in the Late Period. It is much more cursive (joined-up) than hieratic and it is often very difficult to make out individual signs.

By contrast, scribes had the option to detail every feather on bird signs' wings if they were carving on a softer stone such as limestone. Compare these reed leaf hieroglyphs, from the Rosetta Stone (far left) and from a wall inscription on the Temple of Edfu (left).

Different levels of detail were also possible in hieratic texts. Papyri containing the Book of the Dead are written in a cursive hand somewhere between hieroglyphs and hieratic, and it is usually possible to recognize the forms of most signs even if they are simplified in some way (see below).

The tails of snake signs tend to be elongated in cursive hieroglyphs – look how long the tail of the solar snake is on the sign shown below.

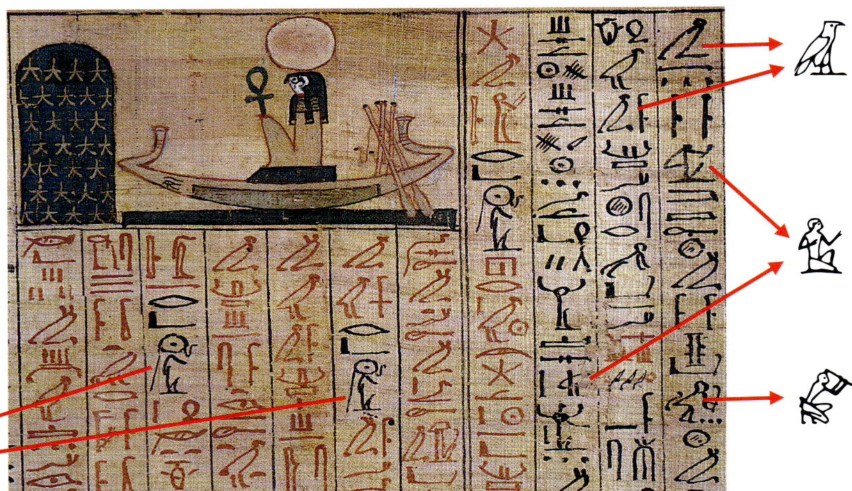

In a fully cursive hieratic text, it is more difficult to relate signs to their hieroglyphic forms, although still sometimes possible (see below).

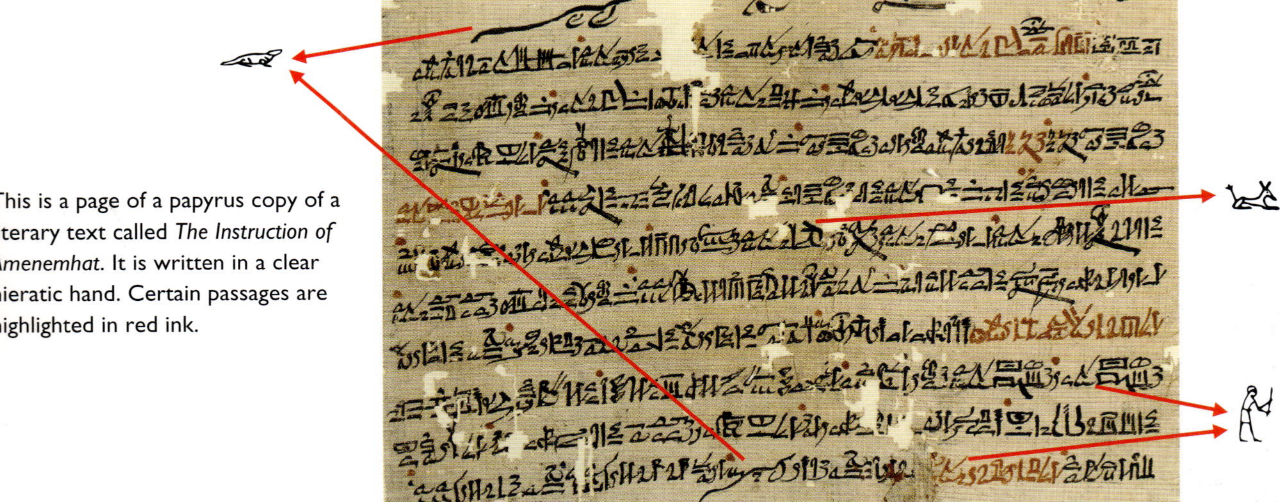

This is a page of a papyrus copy of a literary text called *The Instruction of Amenemhat*. It is written in a clear hieratic hand. Certain passages are highlighted in red ink.

Coptic is the fourth and final type of Egyptian script (alongside hieroglyphic, hieratic, and demotic). It was Egyptian written mainly in Greek characters with some signs added from demotic to represent sounds not present in Greek. Since it includes vowel sounds, it is one of the best ways of working out how Egyptian words might have sounded.

Pottery flake (ostracon) with an inked letter from a bishop in Coptic. 6th century AD.

Putting Ideas into Words – How the Hieroglyphic Script Works

Hieroglyphic signs are usually classified into three categories according to whether they represent *sound*, *meaning*, or both *sound and meaning*.

Sound signs

Hieroglyphs that represent only *sound* are called *phonograms* and can be sub-divided into three further types based on how many consonants they represent: one, two or three. You can see a list of single-consonant signs on page 19. Most words in hieroglyphs are made up of combinations of these sound signs and so are 'spelled out'.

Many words are spelled out with one-consonant sound signs: for example, the word for 'bird' is written with three single-consonant signs: *a* + *p* + *d* (*aped*). But it was common to write a word with a two- or three-consonant sign and then to add one or more single-consonant signs which reinforced the final consonants of the word. Signs used like this are called *sound complements*. For example the most common writing of the word 'offering' (*hetep*) involves three signs: . The offering table sign ( ) is a three-consonant sign and reads *hetep* (*h* + *t* + *p*) by itself, but two single-consonant signs are usually added underneath it to reinforce its last two consonants: is the '*t*'-sound and is the '*p*'. This is not as silly as it may seem at first. A few two- and three-consonant sound signs can be read in more than one way, and so the addition of these extra signs indicates which is the correct reading; for example, the two-consonant sign, (a chisel), can be read either as *ab* or *mer*. Writings with sound complements distinguish between the two: is *ab*, is *mer*. We actually do something similar in English when we write ordinal numbers like 2nd or 3rd. The addition of sound complements (-nd, -rd) tells us to read the numbers as 'second' and 'third' rather than 'two' and 'three'. That we do not read 'twond' and 'threerd' is just a matter of convention. The same applies to sound complements in Egyptian. Any scribe coming across the word would know to read it *hetep* and not *hetepetep*.

Meaning Signs

This hieroglyph showing a bearded deity wearing a tight-fitting shroud acts as a determinative for divine beings. From the coffin of Seni. Middle Kingdom.

The Egyptians usually added one or more *meaning* signs, which we now call *determinatives,* to strings of sound signs. These determinatives were not read aloud as part of the sound of the word, but instead gave an indication of what a word might mean. Thus, the word for 'bird' (*aped*) is usually written with a bird determinative (usually a goose, which was a typical Egyptian bird) after its sound signs: . The way that Egyptian uses meaning signs has parallels in several languages (e.g. Burmese), although there are only a few comparable examples in English, such as the placing of the letters TM after a brand name to indicate that it is a company trademark, or the image of a running figure accompanying the words 'Fire Exit' on signs.

The advantage of using determinatives is that you can see at a glance what sort of word you are reading. Some of the most common ones are listed in the table on page 17.

Determinatives are one of the special features of written Egyptian, and the modern scribe can have a lot of fun with them. They are discussed again in more detail in chapter 5.

Common Determinatives (Meaning Signs)

Determinative	Description	Used for:
	Egyptian man, seated	Male persons, occupations
	Egyptian woman, seated	Female persons, occupations
	Bearded god	Gods
	Animal hide and tail	Animals, anything made of animal skin
	Sycamore tree	Trees
	Walled city with two intersecting streets	Egyptian cities, places
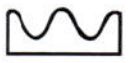	Desert hills	Foreign cities, places
	Papyrus roll	Abstracts – things that can best be described in writing
	Pustule	Moist, soft, bulging things (e.g. wounds)
	Rainy sky	Storms of rain or temper
	Walking legs	Motions like walking, running
	Man with stick	Actions of all kinds

Sound and Meaning Signs

The final way of writing a word in hieroglyphs was to use a sign that represented both *sound and meaning* called a *logogram* (or *ideogram*) which effectively could write a whole word. Thus, the hieroglyphic sign for the sun (☉) writes the word *re* meaning 'sun'. Quite often, logograms are accompanied by a single stroke which is a way of indicating that they are directly representing the word for what they depict: ☉ | . Some common logograms are listed below.

Common Logograms (Sound and Meaning Signs)

Logogram	Description	Egyptian word	Meaning
	Typical boat	*depet*	'Boat'
	Child with finger to mouth	*mes* or *khered*	'Child'
	Ox	*ka* or *ih*	'Ox'
	Stylized house	*per*	'House'
	3 lines of water	*mu*	'Water'
	Brazier alight	*khet*	'Fire'
	Open sail	*tjau*	'Wind; breath'

The three categories of sign described above are not mutually exclusive. Although there are certain hieroglyphs that tend only to fall into one category (e.g. the hide and tail sign, , is only used as a determinative), most signs can play more than one role depending on how they are used. For example, the house sign, , can be a sound sign representing the consonants *p* + *r* in words with nothing to do with houses, a whole-word sign writing the word *per* 'house', and a meaning sign (determinative) in words for any kind of house or dwelling.

Writing Your Name in Hieroglyphs

Despite the differences between the Egyptian script and our Western alphabet, with a bit of creativity you can write the sound of your own name in hieroglyphs using the 22 hieroglyphic signs for the sounds of single consonants. Remember, written ancient Egyptian does not include any of the vowels a, e, i, o, u. You can either omit the vowel sounds in your name completely, like a real ancient Egyptian, or use the approximations given in the list below.

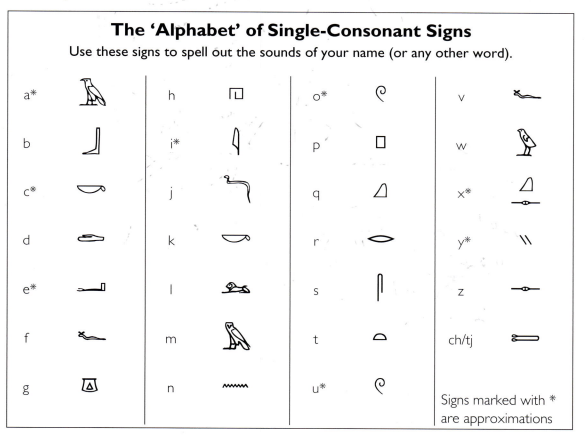

The 'Alphabet' of Single-Consonant Signs

Use these signs to spell out the sounds of your name (or any other word).

a*	 h	o*	v 
b	 i*	 p	w 
c*	 j	 q	x* 
d	 k	 r	 y*
e*	 l	 s	 z 
f	 m	 t	ch/tj 
g	n	 u*	

Signs marked with * are approximations

Helpful hint

Remember that the Egyptians liked to write hieroglyphs as neatly as possible. So put low, broad signs underneath each other, for example:

carolyn

richard

One of the biggest differences between English and Egyptian is the use of determinatives (meaning signs) which can be added to ends of words in Egyptian to sum up their meaning or to give extra information about them. When writing names, the closest equivalent in English is the way we use titles to describe ourselves – Mr, Ms, Dr, and so on – but determinatives can give much more detail. A simple change of determinative can turn an ordinary person into a god!

Examples:

Carolyn (the goddess)

(Sir) Richard

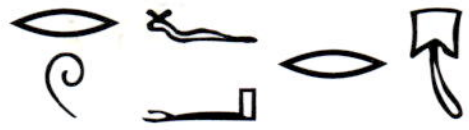

Rover (an animal)

Define Yourself with a Determinative

Add one of these signs to the end of your name to say something about who you are, or how you feel.

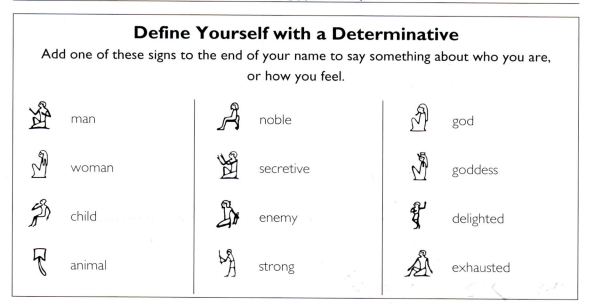

man	noble	god
woman	secretive	goddess
child	enemy	delighted
animal	strong	exhausted

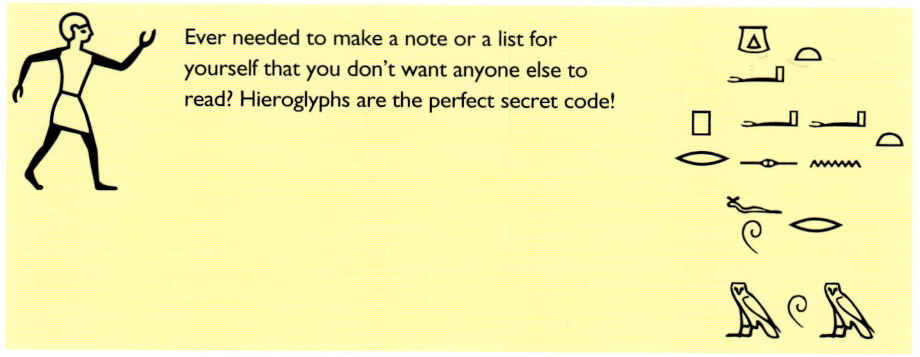

Ever needed to make a note or a list for yourself that you don't want anyone else to read? Hieroglyphs are the perfect secret code!

2 People and their Names

Names as Protection

In the Middle Kingdom story known as *The Tale of Wonders*, the birth of three kings of the 5th Dynasty is described. In the tale, the sun-god Ra was the father of the children and so their birth was attended by the creator god Khnum and four goddesses of childbirth – Isis, Nephthys, Meskhenet and Heket. These deities helped the royal triplets' human mother in her labour, but they also played the important role of giving the children their names. This act of naming takes on a magical aspect in the story. Each child's name reflects a wish for his health and well-being; for example, when Isis delivers the first child, she says: 'Don't be so mighty ([hieroglyphs] *user*) in her womb, you whose name is 'Mighty' ([hieroglyphs] *User*)'. This statement gives the child a powerful name but also magically hastens his birth and protects him.

Although *The Tale of Wonders* is just a story, in real life too the Egyptians chose their children's names very carefully. Mortality rates were particularly high for young children so parents wanted to take every step to ensure their survival. As soon as a child was born, he or she was given a name that could serve as a protection. This could be done in different ways. The most common method was to link the child with a god. A name like *Ramesses* was really a statement in hieroglyphs, meaning 'It is Ra (*Ra*) who gives birth to (*mes*) him (*ses*)'. The name forged a strong connection between the child and Ra which, in the minds of hopeful parents, would encourage the god to look after the child. Many names were composed according to formulae, as you can see in the following chart.

Senmut ('Brother of Mut') with Princess *Neferura* ('The Beauty of Ra'). Both names incorporate those of gods. New Kingdom.

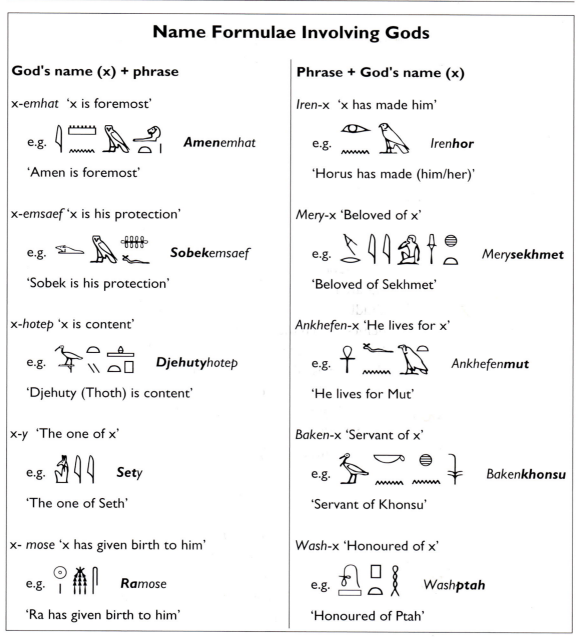

Name Formulae Involving Gods

God's name (x) + phrase	**Phrase + God's name (x)**
x-*emhat* 'x is foremost' e.g. ***Amen****emhat* 'Amen is foremost'	*Iren*-x 'x has made him' e.g. *Iren****hor*** 'Horus has made (him/her)'
x-*emsaef* 'x is his protection' e.g. ***Sobek****emsaef* 'Sobek is his protection'	*Mery*-x 'Beloved of x' e.g. *Mery****sekhmet*** 'Beloved of Sekhmet'
x-*hotep* 'x is content' e.g. ***Djehuty****hotep* 'Djehuty (Thoth) is content'	*Ankhefen*-x 'He lives for x' e.g. *Ankhefen****mut*** 'He lives for Mut'
x-*y* 'The one of x' e.g. ***Set****y* 'The one of Seth'	*Baken*-x 'Servant of x' e.g. *Baken****khonsu*** 'Servant of Khonsu'
x- *mose* 'x has given birth to him' e.g. ***Ra****mose* 'Ra has given birth to him'	*Wash*-x 'Honoured of x' e.g. *Wash****ptah*** 'Honoured of Ptah'

As part of their punishment, criminals like tomb robbers or conspirators would have their names changed so that instead of being 'Loved by (a god)' or 'Praised by (a god)' they became 'Hated by (a god)'. Since the Egyptians believed that the gods controlled life's successes and failures, they took every precaution to keep them happy. In personal names, which are often statements, a god's name will be put right at the beginning, out of the natural grammatical order as a sign of respect ('honorific transposition'). When we read the name, we put the god's name in its proper grammatical place, for example: the name *Irtybastet* ('The Eyes of Bastet') can be split into the words *irty* 'eyes' and the name of the goddess *Bastet*. When it is written, however, the name of the goddess comes first to show deference to her: .

However, names need not always involve a god or a goddess. Some names are parents' wishes for their child, for example:

Menekhibnet 'May (his) property flourish'

Meresankh 'May she love life'

The king was without question the most important living person and his name had to reflect his importance. Kings actually took on four royal names when they ascended to the throne in addition to their birth name. Each had a solemn title and described an aspect of the king's role:

The Horus Name
The Two Ladies Name
The Golden Horus Name
The King of Upper and Lower Egypt Name (throne name)
The Son of Ra Name (birth name)

Most inscriptions only refer to kings by the last two names, although the most formal texts list all five, like the text on the back pillar of the statue of Ramses II (right). His names were:

Horus: Strong Bull, Beloved of Maat
Two Ladies: Protector of Egypt, Curber of Foreign Lands
Golden Horus: Powerful of Years, Great of Successes
King of Upper and Lower Egypt: User-Maat-Ra ('Powerful is the Justice of Ra')
Son of Ra: Ramses ('It is Ra who has given birth to him').

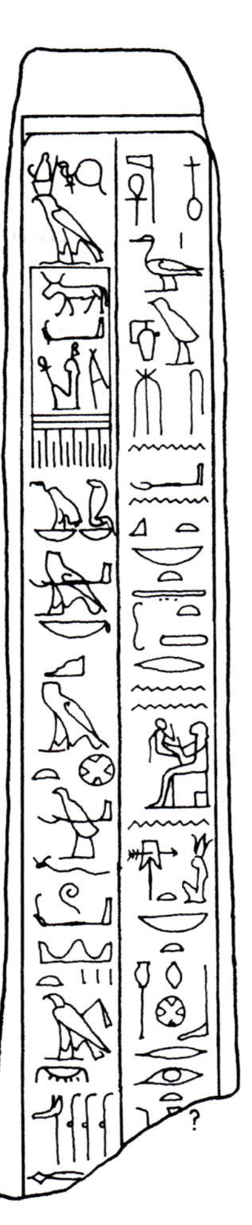

Others are hopeful, confident statements:

Ankhtyfy 'The one who will live'

is an abbreviated version of . Many names employ a kind of 'shorthand' like this.

Wereshunefer 'One who spends the day happy'

A few express similar sentiments but betray a little of the uncertainty that must have haunted parents:

 *Dersenedj* 'The one who wards away fear'

A plucked goose is the usual determinative of *senedj* 'fear', maybe because of its goosebumps?!

Nicknames

It seems as if most Egyptians had a 'grand' name that was used in formal inscriptions and a 'nickname' that might have been used more informally by friends and family. These nicknames were very often abbreviations of the fuller name, for example the man named *Pepyima* ('The Charming One of (King) Pepi') was also known as *Ima* ('Charmer'). But sometimes the nickname was entirely different from the formal name. An official of the Middle Kingdom had the formal name *Ptahemsaef* ('Ptah is his protection') but was named *Senebtyfy* on his statue (right: 'The one who will be healthy').

Statue of Ptahemsaef, nicknamed Senebtyfy. Middle Kingdom.

Indeed sometimes we know men and women only by what may be their more informal names which simply describe characteristics. Some focus on an aspect of physical appearance, for example:

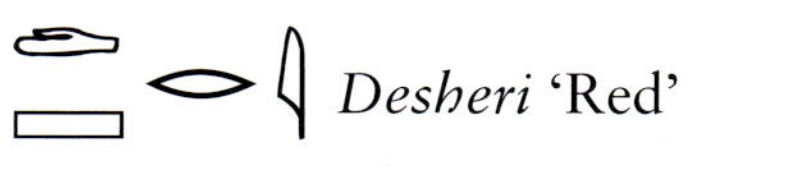 *Desheri* 'Red'

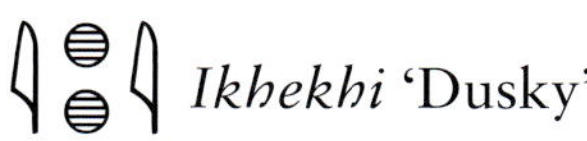 *Ikhekhi* 'Dusky'

 *Anemher* 'Gorgeous'

 *Tjehenet* 'Gleaming'

Other nicknames are simple tokens of affection:

Khenuib 'Heart's treasure' *Bia* 'Miracle'

Webennesiah 'The moon shines for her'

'Fertility plaque' showing a mother embracing her child. New Kingdom.

Some names make the bond between parent and child even more explicit:

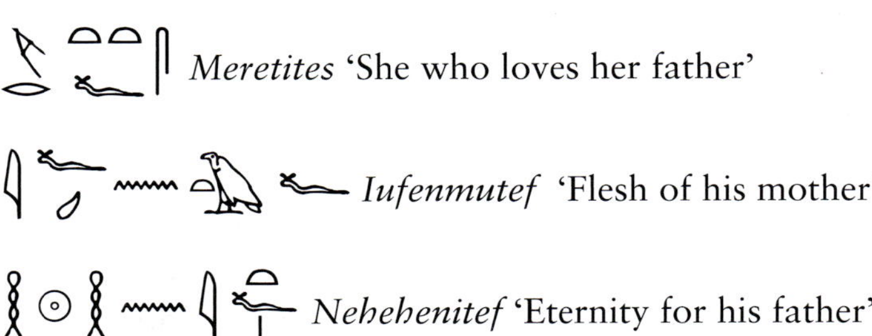

Meretites 'She who loves her father'

Iufenmutef 'Flesh of his mother'

Nehehenitef 'Eternity for his father'

Certain names stand out as being rather unusual and we can only guess at their origins. Did the man called *Seshnu* have soft skin or a sweet smell?

Seshnu 'Waterlilies'

Was the man named *Akhpet* born at dusk?

Akhpet 'The sky darkens'

What about

Sabnes 'Multi-coloured of tongue',

Sebarekhyt 'The star of the common people',

and

Bakennanefu 'Servant of the winds'?

Family Relations

Families were the heart of ancient Egyptian life. The word which we translate as 'family' reinforces this:

abet means 'That which is longed for'.

Since identity was expressed through parentage, we often learn the names of a person's father and mother on stelae he (or sometimes, she) commissioned. The notion of passing on his position in society and family wealth to his children was ingrained in every nobleman's heart. When an inscription was carved on a stela or a tomb wall asking for remembrance and offerings, there was often a blessing and a curse attached. For those who wished the deceased well and said their name aloud, the blessing was that they should pass on their offices to their children. The curse threatened the opposite: those who caused harm would see their family line die out.

Thanks to the Egyptian custom of compiling family lists on stelae, we know most of the terms used to describe family members:

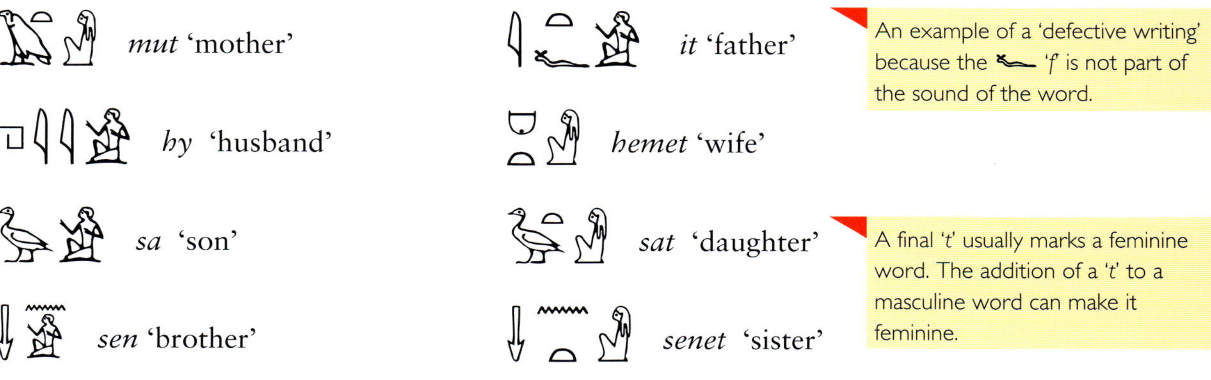

mut 'mother'
it 'father'
hy 'husband'
hemet 'wife'
sa 'son'
sat 'daughter'
sen 'brother'
senet 'sister'
An example of a 'defective writing' because the 'f' is not part of the sound of the word.
A final 't' usually marks a feminine word. The addition of a 't' to a masculine word can make it feminine.

The terms for other relations are built of these basic blocks; for example:

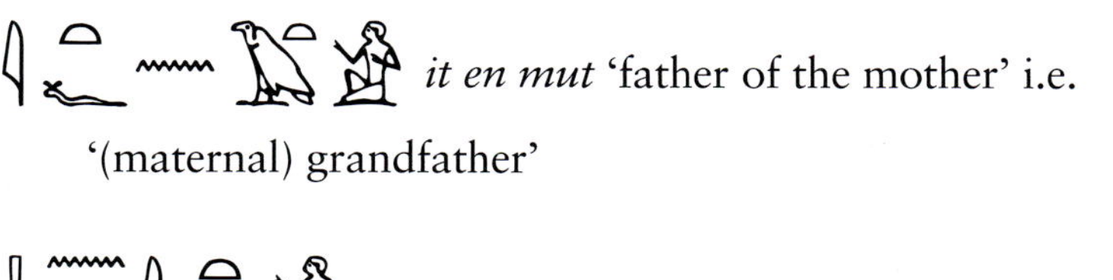

it en mut 'father of the mother' i.e. '(maternal) grandfather'
sen en it 'brother of the father' i.e. 'uncle'

Some terms were used affectionately to describe ties between people who were not necessarily related. Sometimes teachers formed close bonds with their pupils and called them *sa* 'son'. The word *senet* (literally 'sister') was used in love poems for 'beloved'. It became an alternative word for the more formal term *hemet* even in everyday contexts like labels for family on stelae or tomb walls. The masculine equivalent *sen* ('brother') is also found in love poems meaning 'beloved', but not on stelae since they were seldom composed from a woman's perspective.

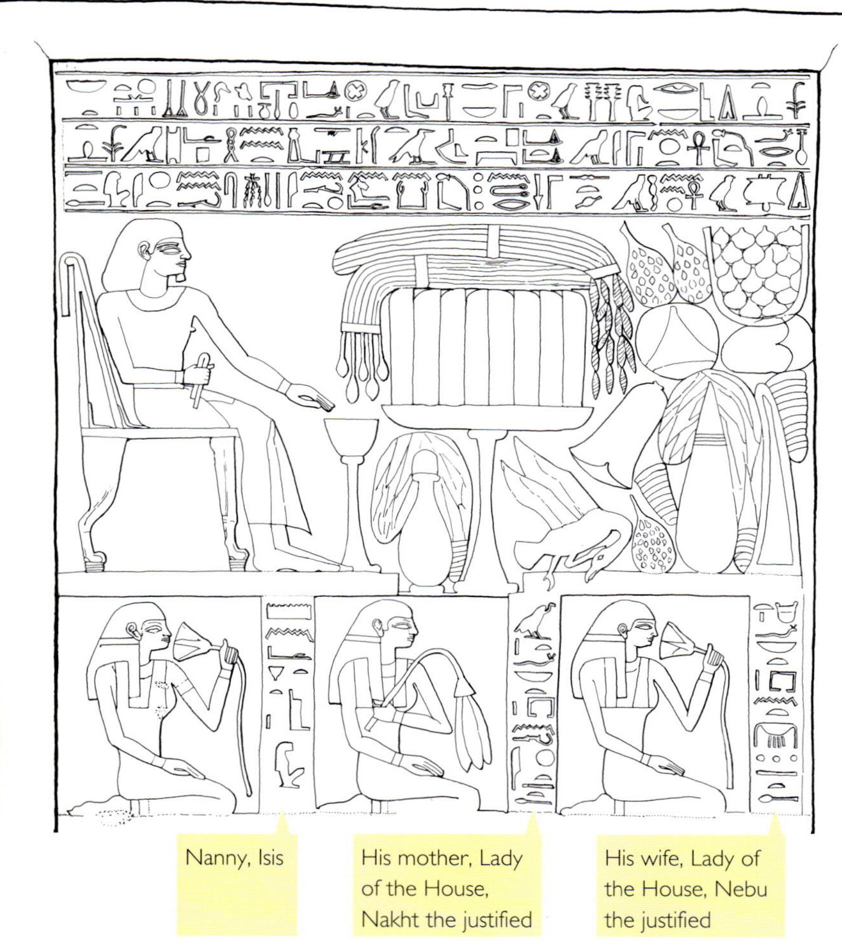

To lists of terms for family members, the Egyptians added *menat* 'wet-nurse' or 'nanny'. Nannies often stayed with families long after their young charges had grown up. On the stela of a man named Nakht (left), the deceased's nanny is depicted (far left, under his chair) alongside his mother and his wife.

The arrangement of relations on stelae can often tell us a lot about family politics. On his stela, the family of a man named Minnefer is depicted making offerings to him. Although he was married, it is his mother who stands behind him in a position of honour. His wife, Henu, is depicted behind Minnefer's sister Hapy and his niece Mutseneter. Continuing the emphasis on his sister's family, Hapy's son Aa is the first male figure in the register below his mother and sister and is given special prominence through his distinctive clothing and the sacrificial ox's foreleg that he holds while all the others hold lotus flowers. Minnefer's father Sobekdedu and maternal grandfather, also called Minnefer, stand behind him.

The arrangement and captioning of the people on this stela tells us that Minnefer inherited his name from his mother's father, and thus that her family line was important. It also tells us that since Minnefer does not seem to have had any children to carry on his own line, the family's continuance has fallen to his sister's children and that his nephew is playing the ritual role (offering the ox's leg) his own son would have performed. Since Henu could not give her husband children, she has been relegated to the background.

Terms of Endearment

The epithet [hieroglyphs] *mery* ([hieroglyphs] *meryt*) 'beloved' was often added to the name of a child, sibling or spouse. This was a suitably formal term to appear alongside family members' images on tomb walls and stelae. Otherwise only a few terms of endearment are known; e.g. [hieroglyphs] *ibib* 'sweetheart' (literally: 'heart of (my) heart'). There are many words to describe close friends:

[hieroglyphs] *meh ib* 'one who fills the heart'

[hieroglyphs] *ak ib* 'one who enters the heart'

There are two writings of the more formal term *semer* 'companion' which was usually applied to the courtiers closest to the king. The first of its two determinatives, , depicts a nobleman holding a staff of office in one hand and a folded cloth in the other, both status symbols. Such companions of the king might be called upon to defend him in times of trouble, and so to bring out this nuance, *semer* could be written with an alternative determinative, a man brandishing a stick: .

Maybe it is because children were the ones who perpetuated the family line that we know of many more terms of endearment for them than for husbands or wives. Bird imagery is often used to describe various stages of childhood and infancy. Children in the womb were described as being *imy suwehet* 'within the egg'. was a special way of writing this in hieroglyphs. When they were born, children were called *tjau* 'hatchlings' or *imyu sesh* 'nestlings'. It is possible that the words *sa* 'son' and *sat* 'daughter' were written deliberately with the bird sign, , and really mean 'chick'.

Undesirables

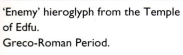

'Enemy' hieroglyph from the Temple of Edfu.
Greco-Roman Period.

Egyptian had many ways of describing various undesirable elements in life. An enemy was *kheruwy*. It is possible to analyse this word in two different ways. It might come from the preposition *kher* 'in front of', which would mean it describes an enemy as 'one who gets in your way'. Or, perhaps more likely, it has its roots in the verb *kher* 'to fall' and so describes enemies as 'ones who (inevitably) fall'. As an alternative to the simple falling man determinative, a more violently graphic alternative was usually used: for example, which shows blood spurting from the head of the falling man, or even which shows the enemy attacking his own head with an axe (see left). The Egyptians believed that once something was given physical shape in art or writing it took on an air of permanence and reality. Thus, the use of these rather macabre enemy determinatives was a magical means of subduing foes.

Words for undesirable states of being or people are particularly interesting for the determinatives they are given, which can sharply hone the nuances of their words. The lock of hair sign seems a strange determinative of words like *khary* 'to be wifeless' and *kharet* 'widow'. To the Egyptians, unbound hair symbolized mourning, since one traditional sign of grief was the act of tearing the hair and throwing dust over it. Thus, the state of being without a spouse is defined as a mournful one.

The word *shemau* is a general term for 'outsiders', or more specifically 'nomads'. It is no coincidence that it can also be used for the personification of illness, 'disease-demons' which the Egyptians believed to be bound up with the movement of foreign peoples. The travelling man determinative, , points to the root of the word, which is the verb *shema* 'to wander'. But *shemau* may be written with a more unusual determinative showing a man hiding his face: . Instead of echoing the root of the word, this sign introduces the idea of the unknown, which the Egyptians always found frightening and threatening.

Occupations

The monuments of noblemen that have come down to us preserve long strings of titles of office and descriptions of professions. The wealthiest members of Egyptian society used two terms of themselves: *haty-a* and *iry-pat* (both written in abbreviated forms) which translate respectively as 'governor' and 'nobleman' and describe administrative authority and high status through birth. Several other titles were used to indicate authority; for example: *hery-tep* 'Chief' and *imy-ra* 'Overseer'. The latter title is usually linked with a specific office: for example,

imy-ra shenut 'Overseer of the Granary'

imy-ra tjebuu 'Overseer of Sandalmakers'

Some of the most important officials in Egypt held the title:

imy-ra kat nebt 'Overseer of All Works' (Boss!)

Such men were in charge of the king's building works; some, like Imhotep the architect of the Step Pyramid Complex at Saqqara, were later worshipped as gods for their achievements.

It is not always clear what duties the holder of certain titles performed, for example:

imy-ra shen ta neb 'Overseer of the hair of every land'

He could have been the first known international hairdresser, or, since *shen* can mean 'pelt, fur', the designer of exotic clothing.

Most titles are written in 'shorthand' with the minimum number of signs because they were so common. There was an even shorter way to write 'overseer': since *imy-ra* literally means 'the one who is in the mouth' (meaning that overseers are mouthy!), the title could be written simply with the tongue sign .

Some professional titles can be broken down into explanations of what their holder did. A sculptor was *sankh*: 'one who makes (things) come to life'. A dentist was known as *ibehy* 'the toothy one'. *sehty* 'farmer' meant 'one who dwells in the countryside'.

Most occupational titles were written with the ordinary male or female determinative:

bak 'servant'

baket 'maidservant'

hemuu 'craftsman'

rekhtyt 'washerwoman'

However, some titles had specific determinatives which summarized in an image the duties their holders might perform or the tools of their trade:

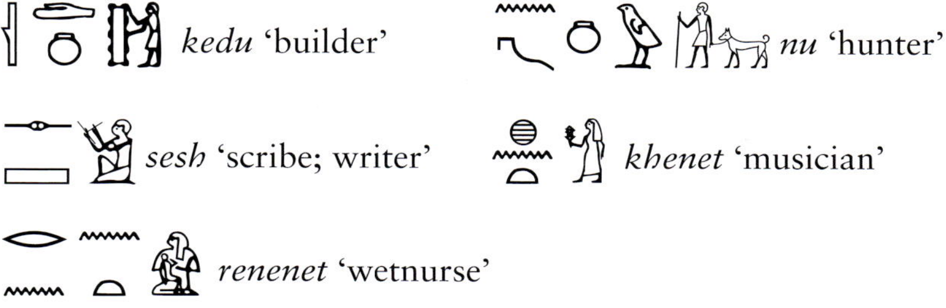

kedu 'builder'

nu 'hunter'

sesh 'scribe; writer'

khenet 'musician'

renenet 'wetnurse'

The Egyptians believed that the more titles someone held, the more important he appeared to be, so sometimes long-obsolete titles were added to functional ones to 'pad out' a nobleman's funerary resumé. Even titles which are genuine sometimes make us wonder exactly what duties were connected with them, especially the following:

hery-seshta en per duat

'Master of Secrets of (the King's) Bathroom'

The Egyptians did not believe that 'less is more'. In the time of Ramses II, a man named Prehotep acted as northern vizier. He left behind two stelae detailing the many titles he held during his lifetime, some of which seem rather fantastic. Here are just a few of them:

> *'Nobleman, Chief of the Two Lands, God's Father beloved of the god, Keeper of Secrets in the Temple of Neith, Confidant of Horus (i.e. the King) in the horizon of eternity, Mouth of the King in the Entire Land, Curtain of the Land, Dignitary, Mouth of Nekhen, High priest of Maat, Fanbearer on the right of the King, Overseer of Memphis; Overseer of Priests, Controller of All Kilts; Mouth of the King in Every Foreign Land'*

Make Up Your Own Egyptian Name

You can invent an Egyptian name for yourself or for a friend by following the guidelines below. Just pick an adjective to describe yourself from column A on page 35. So you could be

User 'The Mighty One'

or *An* 'The Gorgeous One'.

Or, if you really want your name to make a statement, combine an adjective from column A with one of the words from column B. You could be

User ka 'Powerful of Spirit'

or *An shen* 'The One with Gorgeous Hair'!

Don't forget to add a determinative at the end to say whether you're male ( ), female ( ), divine (: see page 37 for more divine determinatives), or an animal ( )!

Create Your Own Egyptian Name

Choose a description from column A, and combine it with a word from column B for maximum impact.

A: Adjectives

An 'Gorgeous'

Asha 'Abundant'

Bin 'Wicked'

Wer 'Great (of)'

Nefer 'Beautiful'

User 'Powerful'

Hedj 'Dazzling'

Nedjem 'Sweet'

Kened 'Furious'

Wab 'Pure'

Nedjes 'Short (of)'

Tekh 'Tipsy'

Ken 'Brave'

B: Nouns

henket 'beer'

resut 'dreams'

iamut 'charm'

her 'face'

a 'arm'

khet 'body'

sebehyt 'laughter'

ka 'spirit'

shen 'hair'

reduwy 'legs'

ib 'heart'

ra 'mouth'

seshtau 'secrets'

3 Gods and their Names

The Gods of Ancient Egypt

One of the characteristic features of ancient Egyptian society was its religious devotion. The Egyptians strongly believed that divine forces had not only shaped the world, but also continued to influence everyday matters. Gods surrounded them: the sun, the sky, the earth, and especially the annual, life-giving flooding of the Nile known as the Inundation – all of these were imagined as divinities. Each town had a patron god or goddess, sometimes more than one. Some deities had magnificent temples built for them by kings, others were worshipped at humble shrines within private households. Since the gods were such an important part of Egyptian life, their names were imbued with meaning and often can tell us something of a deity's origins or character. This chapter explores various names that the Egyptians assigned to the divine realm. Where the commonly-used English versions of gods' names differ from the original Egyptian, an indication of the latter is given.

Signs of Divinity

As discussed above, determinatives (meaning signs added to the ends of words) had the power to change the nature of the word with which they were written. This is especially true of divine determinatives. There were four special determinatives that were used with the names of deities, each capturing the idea of divinity in a different way.

The scribe Hunefer (left) worshipping the gods. New Kingdom.

Divine Determinatives

Sign	Description	Used for:
	Bearded god	All male deities
	Divine falcon on a perch	All deities
	Rearing cobra (uraeus)	All goddesses
( )	Woman with (or without) uraeus	All goddesses

One more hieroglyph is specifically connected to deities: the sign . This represented a tall pole with a flag attached of the kind that would have stood outside a typical Egyptian temple and so was a recognizable, outward sign of divinity. Occasionally this sign was also used as a determinative for the names of gods and goddesses.

Names for Gods and of Gods

According to ancient Egyptian belief, the divine realm was populated not only with full-scale gods and goddesses, but also with a whole host of minor deities or 'demons'. Major gods were known as *netjer* (*netjeret* 'goddess'). But there were different terms for these lesser deities, such as *sekhem* 'powerful one' or *nebed* 'evil one'. The determinative (meaning sign) of *nebed* is telling: represents a lock of hair and may be a way of indicating that this type of being is more animal (i.e. hairy!) than human.

Deities' names could be spelled out with sound signs (phonograms) accompanied by one of the determinatives shown above. There was also an abbreviated way of writing the god's name with a single sign (a logogram, which has both sound and meaning), usually using the god's sacred animal (see chart on page 38.)

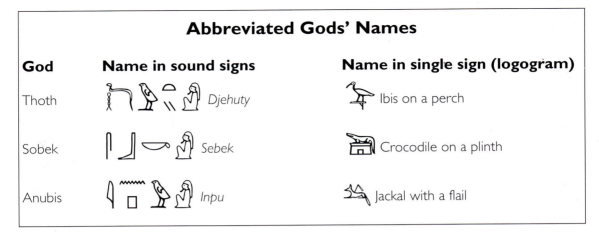

Abbreviated Gods' Names

God	Name in sound signs	Name in single sign (logogram)
Thoth	*Djehuty*	Ibis on a perch
Sobek	*Sebek*	Crocodile on a plinth
Anubis	*Inpu*	Jackal with a flail

Writings using a sacred animal logogram (a sign combining sound and meaning and therefore a word in itself) had a great deal of potency and they were used carefully. There were certain sensitive religious texts which were designed to be in close proximity to the person who would make use of them: for example, the Pyramid Texts on the walls of a king's burial chambers or the Coffin Texts carved or painted onto the interior of a non-royal coffin. So in the case of deities like the aggressive crocodile-god Sobek or the violent god of chaos Seth, divine names were often written with sound signs in such texts to avoid any danger from the animal icons: thus, (*S-b-k* 'Sobek') and (*S-t-sh* 'Seth') instead of and . In the case of evil demi-gods, like the giant snake Apophis (*Apep*) who attacked the boat of the sun-god each night in the Underworld, measures could be taken to restrain their evil influence when writing their names. The snake determinative of names for Apophis usually had knives stuck into it.

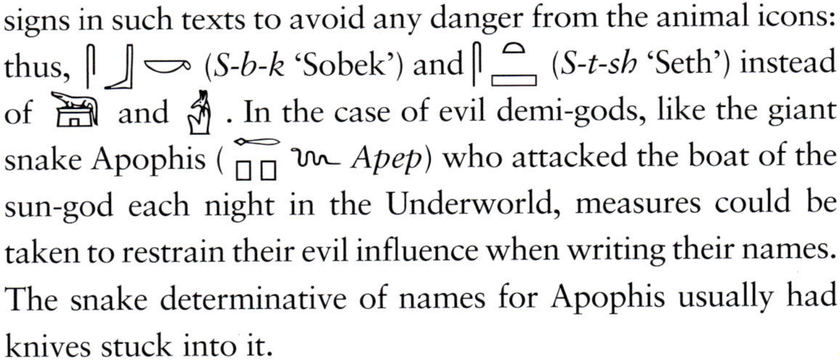

On the walls of the Temple of Edfu Apophis is described as *Denden* 'The Furious One' – the snake determinative has been mutilated with knives.
Greco-Roman Period.

The name of Seth caused a dilemma for King Sety I, who was named after this god. Usually his name (meaning 'Man of Seth') was written with a Seth deity sign: . However, at his temple in Abydos, he must have felt that even a hieroglyphic Seth might offend Seth's divine brother Osiris, the patron god of the city (in Egyptian mythology, Seth had murdered Osiris). So Sety replaced the offending sign in his name with a more generic god sign, , which happens to bear a resemblance to Osiris himself. Occasionally, Sety used another sign entirely, a so-called Isis knot, , perhaps in an attempt to curry favour with Osiris' wife, Isis?

The Gods of Creation

The names of those gods and goddesses connected with creation are usually easy to interpret since they tend to represent some essence of the creative process. In Egypt, there was not just one version of the creation of the world. Each city told its own myth describing the beginnings of life known as a cosmogony. According to the city of Hermopolis, the creation of the world came about through eight primeval deities, four gods and four goddesses, who represented the male and female sides of four forces of nature: Darkness, Eternity, Formlessness and Hiddenness. Amun ('Hiddenness') evolved away from these abstract and rather murky beginnings and by the New Kingdom was hailed as 'the King of the Gods'.

[hieroglyph] shows the sky ([hieroglyph]) resting precariously on a broken support – the Egyptians thought of darkness as the falling of the sky.

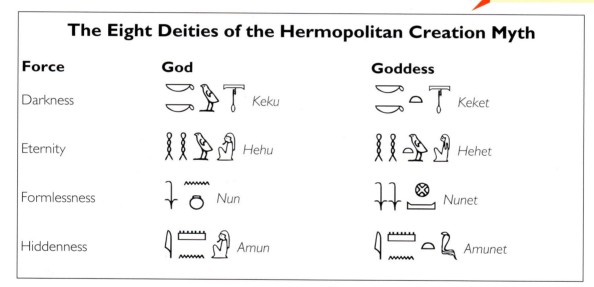

The Eight Deities of the Hermopolitan Creation Myth

Force	God	Goddess
Darkness	[hieroglyphs] *Keku*	[hieroglyphs] *Keket*
Eternity	[hieroglyphs] *Hehu*	[hieroglyphs] *Hehet*
Formlessness	[hieroglyphs] *Nun*	[hieroglyphs] *Nunet*
Hiddenness	[hieroglyphs] *Amun*	[hieroglyphs] *Amunet*

In Memphis, a different story was told in which the craftsman god Ptah simply called to mind the elements of the world and then spoke their names to bring them into being. This emphasizes the life-giving quality of names. Although he is the sole creator in the Memphite creation myth, some versions of the myth personify his thoughts and words into gods: [hieroglyphs] *Sia* 'Perception' and [hieroglyphs] *Hu* 'Utterance'. However, they would never have been worshipped independently. By contrast, Ptah was one of the longest-lived and most important deities in Egypt. He was the patron god of Memphis, which was the administrative capital throughout most of Egyptian history, and he had a magnificent temple complex there which sadly has not survived. It is not certain what his name originally meant, but it was later used as a verb, *peteh*, meaning 'to create, fashion'.

One of the oldest myths was associated with the ancient city of Heliopolis and centred around a creator-god called Atum. His name, *Item*, means 'The Complete One', and acknowledges that from Atum alone sprang the first pair of deities through whom the first elements of the world come into being: *Shu* 'Air' and *Tefnut* 'Moisture'. These two gods in turn generate a second pair of deities who give further shape to the developing world: *Geb* 'Earth' and *Nut* 'Sky'.

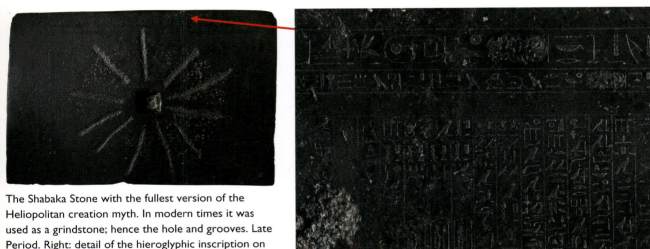

The Shabaka Stone with the fullest version of the Heliopolitan creation myth. In modern times it was used as a grindstone; hence the hole and grooves. Late Period. Right: detail of the hieroglyphic inscription on the stone.

From the union of these two deities, four more 'human' gods are born. Isis (*Aset* 'Throne') and her sister *Nephthys* (*Nebethut* 'Lady of the House') are stabilizing influences for the tempestuous relationship that exists between their brothers. Osiris and Seth represent the powerful forces of love and jealousy. The names of the two gods are difficult to interpret. Seth (*Setesh*) seems to derive from the verb *setesh* 'to force apart', so that his name means something like 'Outsider'. His name was so powerful that certain texts avoid using it. In the Coffin Texts, a collection of spells to lend magical aid in the Afterlife, scribes often used an epithet for Seth instead: *Wedja* seems to mean something similar to Seth's name – 'The One who Stands Apart'.

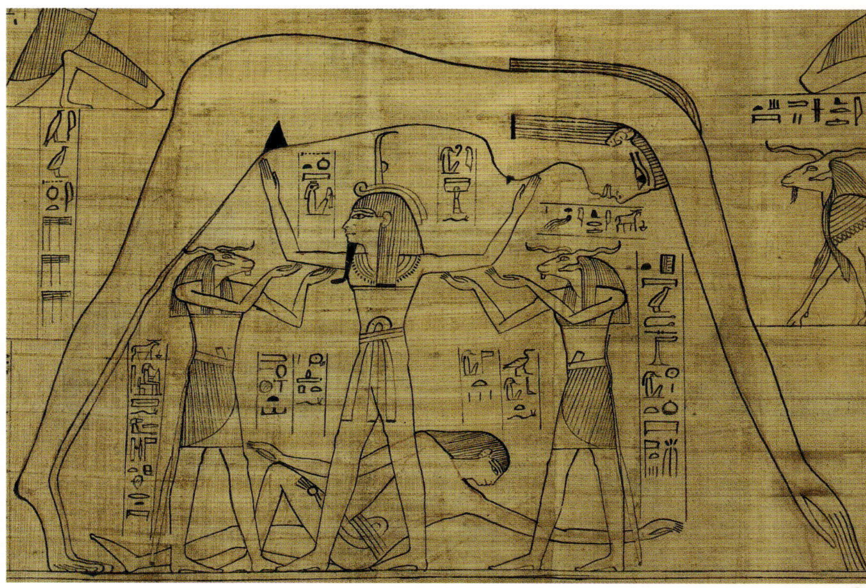

Scene of Shu (the air) separating his children Geb (the earth) and Nut (the sky).
Third Intermediate Period.

The meaning of Osiris' name, *Asir*, is much more controversial and it has been interpreted in a number of different ways. Some have assumed that the traditional writing with the throne and the eye is a hidden (or cryptographic) writing of *User* 'The Powerful One'. Others take the signs with which his name is written as the words *aset* 'throne' and *iri* 'to make, do, act', interpreting their combination as 'He who occupies the throne' or 'He whom Isis (The Throne) has made'. It may be that the Egyptians themselves deliberately kept the origins of Osiris' name shrouded in mystery through abbreviated writings out of respect for the secrecy of the god's cult. Other important gods, like Anubis (*Inpu*) and Thoth (*Djehuty*), have names that are not easily interpreted. It may be that certain divine names were very ancient and that in time even the Egyptians forgot what they meant.

Gods of the Natural World

Like Shu, Tefnut, Geb and Nut, several Egyptian gods represented physical elements of the world, including the supreme deity of Egypt, the falcon-headed god Ra, whose name meant 'Sun' and was written either with a sun-disc determinative after sound signs ☉ or just with the sun-disc itself: ☉ . It is difficult to tell whether the sun was named after the god, or vice versa. Certain gods can be seen as deifications of natural phenomena; for example, the Egyptians made a careful distinction between the Nile, which they called *iteru* 'River', and the life-giving Inundation which made agriculture possible for them. The Inundation was envisaged as a god called *Hapi* whose name meant 'Flood'.

The most important personification of a natural force was the goddess *Maat*. The key element in her name is the ostrich feather: .

The jackal god Anubis weighing the heart of a nobleman while the demon Ammut ('She who eats the dead') awaits the outcome. New Kingdom.

In art, Maat wears this feather on her head, but the feather alone could represent her presence and essence. Thus, when the deceased has his heart weighed in the Hall of Judgement, the feather of Maat is often shown not only in one of the scale pans, but also on the top of the scales themselves (see left).

The concept of Maat is extremely complex. The Egyptians used the term to describe the vital balance between all the opposing elements in the universe – good and evil, light and dark, life and death. When translated into English, it has a wide spectrum of meanings: truth, righteousness, justice, cosmic harmony. Ironically, despite her importance, the goddess Maat did not have temples of her own. Yet she is present in the decoration of almost every Egyptian temple; most commonly in scenes where the Pharaoh presents a small image of her to the gods as a symbol of his just conduct.

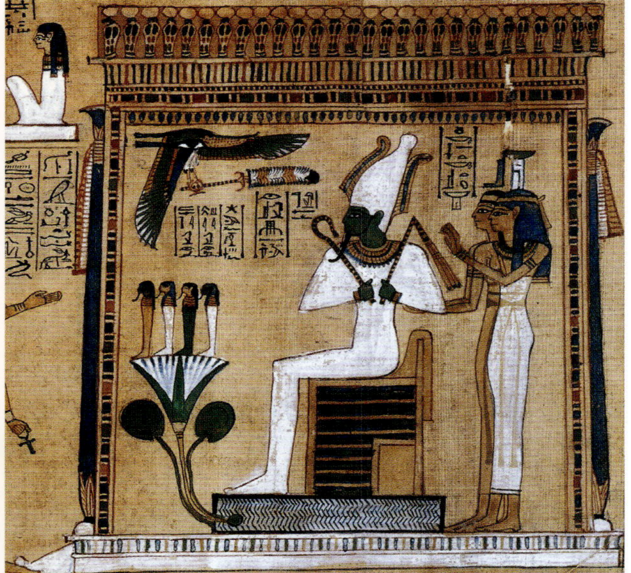

Two goddesses Isis and Nephthys stand behind Osiris, wearing their special signs on their heads. New Kingdom.

Certain gods wear the hieroglyphs for their names on their heads like crowns, perhaps as a way of strengthening their identity and presence (see left).

Gods and their Sacred Animals

A different way of identifying gods was through their sacred animal. In art, gods and goddesses could be shown in human form, or with a human body and the head of their sacred animal. Sometimes, they could take full animal shape. It seems as if the connection between deity and sacred animal was so strong that the deity's name could be used for the animal; for example, *sebek* can mean either a divine crocodile or the crocodile-god Sobek. The god Thoth, whose Egyptian name *Djehuty* may mean 'The Ibis', was also known as *Fendjy* 'The Nosey One' because of the ibis' long beak.

It is possible that the fierce goddess *Taweret* got her name, which simply means 'The Great One', from her animal components. She is usually represented as a pregnant hippopotamus baring her sharp teeth in a menacing grin. It seems as if this was not always intimidating enough for the Egyptians, for sometimes the goddess has the tail of a crocodile too. Despite her formidable appearance, Taweret was a protectress of the vulnerable, particularly mothers and children. Similarly, the goddess of war and plague *Sekhmet*, whose name means 'The Powerful One' no doubt drew some inspiration for her name from her sacred animal, the lioness.

Faience statuette of Taweret. New Kingdom.

The falcon-headed god Horus was the divine child of Osiris and Isis. His name seems to be connected to his sacred animal: *Her*, means 'The Distant One' and seems to evoke the height at which the falcon can soar in the sky. It could be written with the falcon sign, or with sound signs and the road determinative ( ) which represents the idea of distance: .

Demons and Demi-gods

The Egyptians imagined a whole host of semi-divine beings of a more ambiguous temperament. Many such beings guarded the Gates of the Underworld and had to be sweet-talked into letting a deceased person pass on into the Afterlife. Some demons' names tell us of their origins:

Demons with knives guarding a gate of the Underworld. New Kingdom.

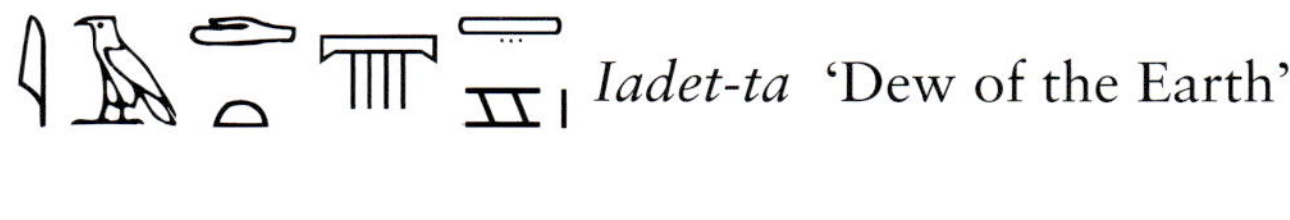

Iadet-ta 'Dew of the Earth'

Ibib-ta 'Earth's Darling'

Mostly their names reflect their fearful and mysterious natures:

Iuti-her-ef 'The One without a Face'

Itji-em-gereh 'The One who Seizes in the Night'

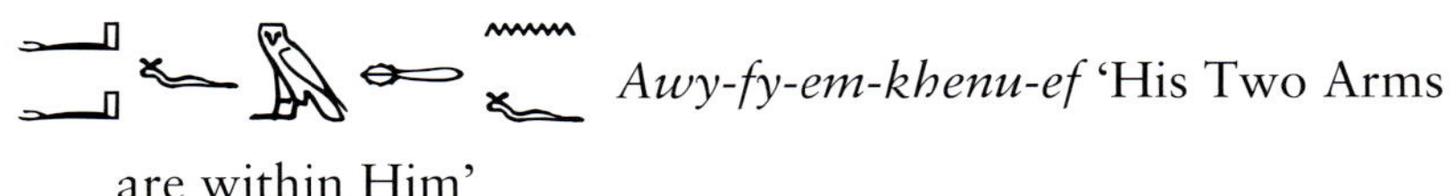 *Awy-fy-em-khenu-ef* 'His Two Arms are within Him'

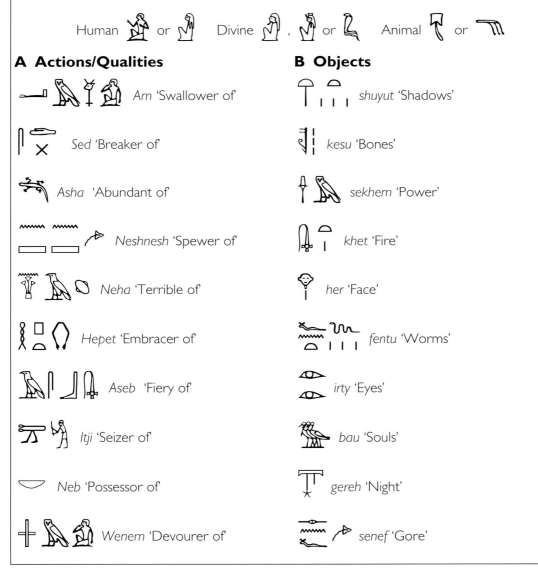

Ikhemu-hemy-ef 'The One who Knows no Turning Back'.

Create Your Own Demonic Name

You can make up your own demonic name by combining an action or quality from column A with an object from column B. You could add a determinative for further characterization; for example:

Human or Divine , or Animal or

A Actions/Qualities

Am 'Swallower of'

Sed 'Breaker of'

Asha 'Abundant of'

Neshnesh 'Spewer of'

Neha 'Terrible of'

Hepet 'Embracer of'

Aseb 'Fiery of'

Itji 'Seizer of'

Neb 'Possessor of'

Wenem 'Devourer of'

B Objects

shuyut 'Shadows'

kesu 'Bones'

sekhem 'Power'

khet 'Fire'

her 'Face'

fentu 'Worms'

irty 'Eyes'

bau 'Souls'

gereh 'Night'

senef 'Gore'

Divine Places

When the Egyptians constructed buildings they always named them. The largest temple complex in Egypt, Karnak in Thebes, was called *Ipet-isut* 'The Choicest of Places'. Instead of the usual building determinative ( ), it has a city determinative ( ).

Typical nobleman's house. New Kingdom. It is very likely that the Egyptians named their houses, although the names do not survive.

Names describing sacred space like temples for the worship of gods or for the deceased king were especially important. Royal 'mortuary' temples were built for the king's funerary cult; their Egyptian name tells us how the Egyptians characterized their purpose; they are called 'Temples of Millions of Years'. Each king's temple had a unique name; below are a few examples from Thebes, the religious capital of Egypt from the New Kingdom.

Royal Funerary Temples and their Names

Temple of	Egyptian Name	Meaning
Amenhotep I	*Men-isut*	'Enduring of Place'
Hatshepsut	*Djeser-djeseru*	'Holy of Holies'
Ramses II	*Khnemet-Waset*	'United with Thebes'
Ramses III	*Khnemet-neheh*	'United with Eternity'

The Egyptians had a multitude of names to describe the heavenly realms of the Afterlife, many of which drew upon solar imagery since the Egyptians believed that the cycle of life was much like the eternal cycle of the sun. Thus, you were buried in *Imentet* 'The West', i.e. the place where the sun of your life set. But your spirit lived on in the *Duat* 'Underworld', the name of which seems to be connected to words for 'dawn' and 'morning'. Thus, in the Underworld, your sun rose again.

Cryptographic (or hidden) writings were often used for temples' names. One effect was sometimes to personify the temple to emphasize that it was a living entity. The image above is a cryptographic writing of the name of one of the temples listed in the table – can you work out which one?

The scribe Ani and his wife enjoying the shade of trees and a cool drink of water in the Afterlife. New Kingdom.

It was also common for the Egyptians to draw on agricultural imagery when they thought about the life that awaited them after death. One of the recurring images of Paradise is called *Sekhet iaru* 'Field of Reeds', where crops grew in abundance after little effort and where tall trees offered plenty of shade from the sun's heat.

Name Your Own Sacred Space

You can create a name for your own home or workplace using the lists below by combining a place name from column A with an attribute from column B:

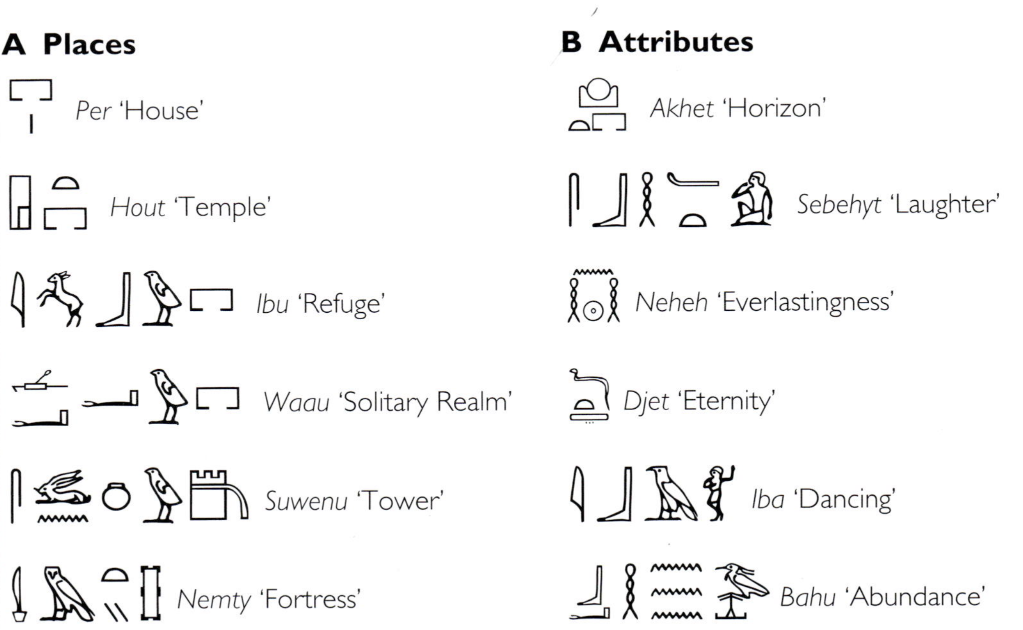

Remember, you could add your name to make the space really yours (see name table on page 19), for example:

 *Nemty Margaret* 'The fortress (of) Margaret'

4 Animals and their Names

Animal Names and Epithets

Animals were present in almost every aspect of daily life in Egypt. Dogs accompanied their masters on hunting trips while cats kept houses safe from unwanted invaders like snakes and rats. Both dogs and cats were common pets, alongside gazelles and monkeys, and lived close to humans. Cattle, sheep, goats and donkeys were vital to agriculture. Other animals like the crocodile and the hippopotamus made life dangerous. Every animal had a role in the Egyptian world, and many of the names the Egyptians gave them tell us something about that role.

Common Egyptian Animals' Names

We learn the names of most of the animals that were familiar to the Egyptians either from mentions in texts or from captioned scenes in art. However, there are still a few animals whose Egyptian names we do not know: for example, butterflies (right) are common in marsh scenes, but in no scene or text are they named.

When writing an animal's name it was common for a scribe to use a non-specific meaning sign (determinative) – something that could apply to various animals – thus saving time and effort: i.e. 𓄛 for animals with a hide and tail; 𓅭 for birds; 𓆛 for fish; 𓆙 for snakes.

However, if the text was an important royal inscription, or if the animal itself was considered to be important, a more specific sign could be used to mark its individuality. There are both specific and generic determinatives in the list on page 48.

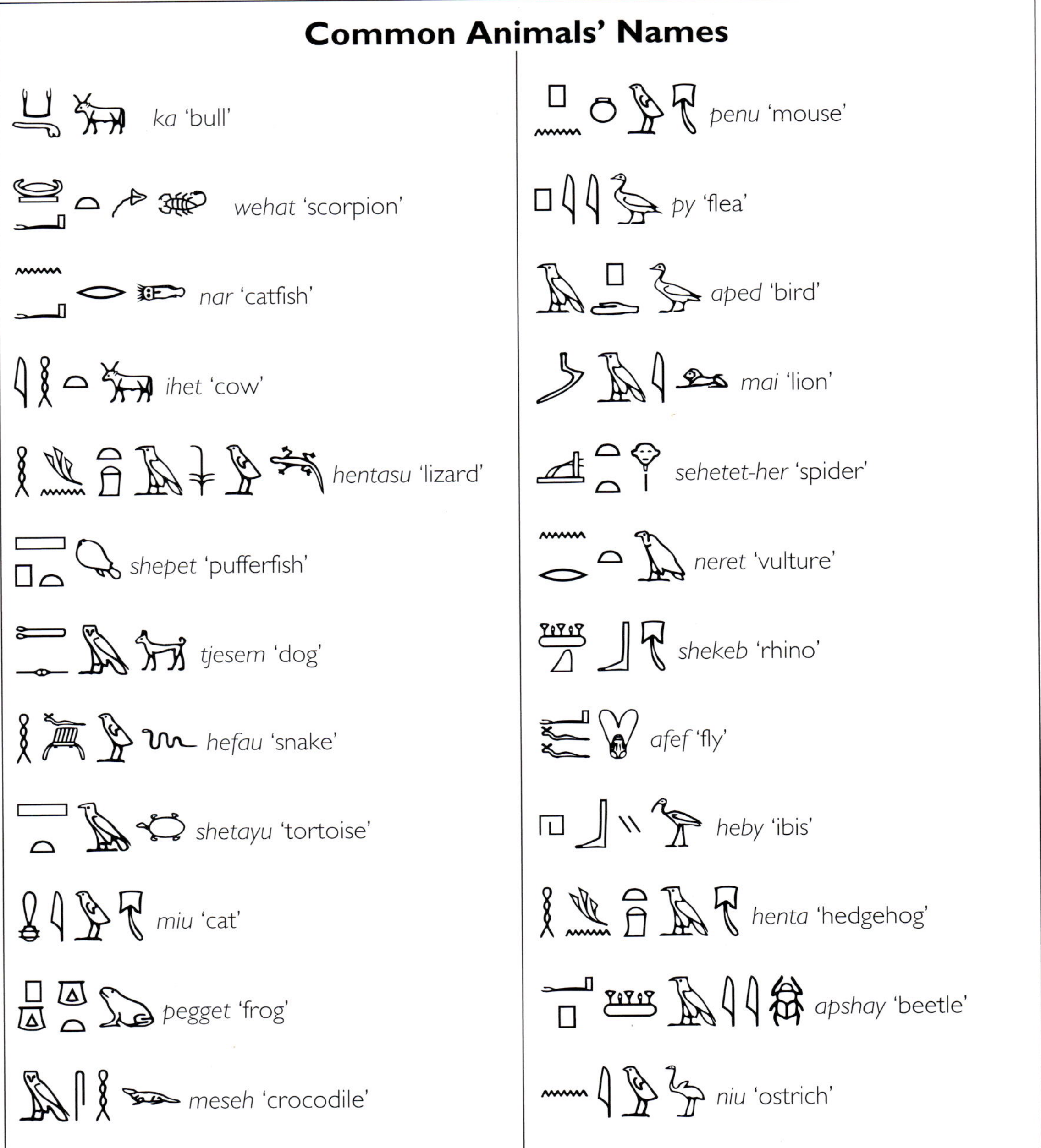

Common Animals' Names
ka 'bull'
wehat 'scorpion'
nar 'catfish'
ihet 'cow'
hentasu 'lizard'
shepet 'pufferfish'
tjesem 'dog'
hefau 'snake'
shetayu 'tortoise'
miu 'cat'
pegget 'frog'
meseh 'crocodile'
penu 'mouse'
py 'flea'
aped 'bird'
mai 'lion'
sehetet-her 'spider'
neret 'vulture'
shekeb 'rhino'
afef 'fly'
heby 'ibis'
henta 'hedgehog'
apshay 'beetle'
niu 'ostrich'

Many of the words listed above are simply the names of animals and have no further meaning; for example, *tjesem* seems only to mean 'dog' and does not seem to indicate a quality or characteristic of the animal (unlike *iuiu* which is a more affectionate name for the same animal – see below). However, certain animal names came to be used more widely: for example, *shepet* 'pufferfish' can be used as a verb meaning 'to be furious', literally to be inflated with anger like a pufferfish.

The most important animals were known by several names: for example, over seventy names are known for various types of cattle. Some are described by their colour, for example:

kem 'black' *desheret* 'red'

sabet 'dappled'

Others are named for their purpose, for example:

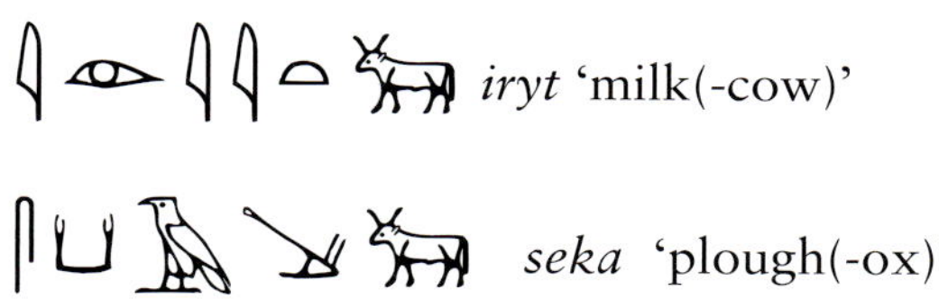

iryt 'milk(-cow)'

seka 'plough(-ox)'

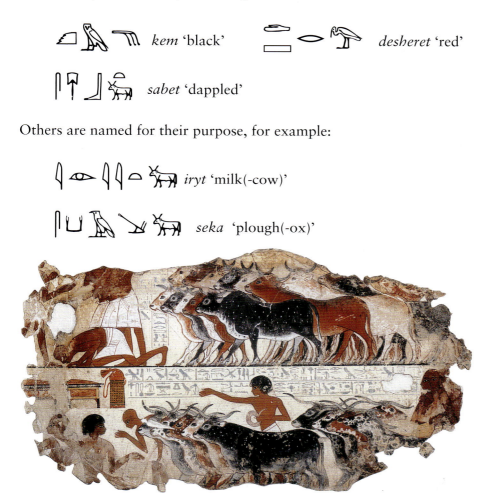

Fragment from the tomb of the nobleman Nebamun showing his cattle being counted. Each is depicted as an individual in a very realistic way.
New Kingdom.

The crocodile also had many names, but for different reasons. The much-feared reptile is mentioned in a variety of different texts both as an animal and as a metaphor. The ordinary name for a crocodile was *meseh*, but it was more common, especially in literary texts, to use an epithet that would recall a particular crocodilian characteristic, for example:

suy 'the dangerous one'

[hieroglyphs] *merytu* 'the bank-dwellers'

Usually, the epithet is carefully chosen to suit the context. The Old Kingdom literary text known as *The Instruction of Ptahhotep* is a wise man's advice to his son about proper living. It includes a warning that things are not always as rosy as they may seem:

> 'No quarrel has ever arisen in the midst of praise,
> but just as the crocodile surfaces, so resentment emerges.'

The word for 'crocodile' in this passage is [hieroglyphs] *kapu* which means 'the hidden one'. Through the use of this epithet, the text creates a powerful image of resentment lurking below the surface of praise just as a crocodile hides itself beneath the water but may appear at any moment.

Detail of the lower part of the stela of Pataweret showing the god Wepwawet helping him to escape from the jaws of a crocodile. It is very likely that the crocodile symbolizes a desperate moment in Pataweret's life when his prayers were answered. New Kingdom.

In royal inscriptions, the king's enemies were often described as crocodiles: treacherous and dangerous. But Queen Hatshepsut used crocodile imagery in a very different way: she described herself as a crocodile four times in her Red Chapel Inscription at Karnak Temple, each time using a different crocodilian epithet. The effect is quite startling:

> 'I am an aggressor ([hieroglyphs] *adu*) who seizes through strength,
> who seizes absolutely, from whose clutches no one can be rescued.
> I am an encircler ([hieroglyphs] *sheny*), who steals opportunities,

who sails upon the water that no one else can navigate.
Indeed I am a lurker (*kapu*), a glider (*depy*),
a raiser of shadows, who is concealed within the shelter.'

Many animals' names were based on those animal's characteristics. Some names are onomatopoeic, and imitate the sound the animal makes, for example:

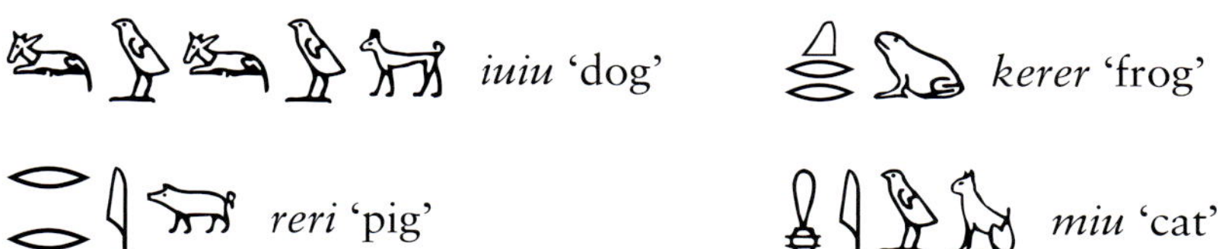

The pet cat of the nobleman Nebamun.
New Kingdom.

Birds were often named on the basis of observations the Egyptians made. The bittern was called *kapu* 'the hidden one' because of its secretive behaviour; the egret was called *seda* 'the trembler' because of its distinctive habit of shaking its head; and the flamingo was named *desher* 'the red one' for its fiery colour. Fish could also be named for their behaviour: schools of fish can be called *fetetu* 'leapers' or *mehyu* 'swimmers'.

Drawing broken lines around the bird hieroglyph's head is a clever way of suggesting that it is shaking!

Even insects could be named for characteristics. Again, they could be named for the sounds they made: the wasp was called *baybay* and the fly *afef* which means 'the buzzing one'. The Egyptians' name for mosquitoes, which must have been just as much of a plague in ancient times as they are now, was chosen with more than a touch of irony – they are called *khenmesu* 'the friendly ones'.

Humans and the Animal World

Since animals were such good representatives of character traits, people often bore animal names as nicknames. We know of several men nicknamed *Wenesh* 'Wolf' and ladies called *Mesehet* 'Crocodile', no doubt tokens of their bearers' fearsomeness. You have to wonder about those called *Penu*, 'Mouse'. Did they choose this name for themselves?

There are many other crossovers between the human and animal worlds. The oldest son in a family could be called *wetu* 'cub', a term usually applied to young foxes. Similarly, in the New Kingdom, an affectionate term for a royal child was *inpu* 'pup', a word derived from the name of the canine god Anubis.

Names for certain parts of animals are also often borrowed from human words and vice versa; for example, an elephant's trunk is called *djeret* in Egyptian, which is the word for a human hand: . *khepesh* means the 'foreleg (of a bull)', but it can also be used to describe the strong arm of a human being, or more abstractly just 'strength' or 'might'. The word for a bird's wing, *djeneh*, is particularly versatile: it can also describe the upper part of a human arm and the rudder-blade of a ship. On a deeper level of language, many of the determinatives (meaning signs) and logograms (sound and meaning signs) for words describing parts of the human body are actually animal rather than human:

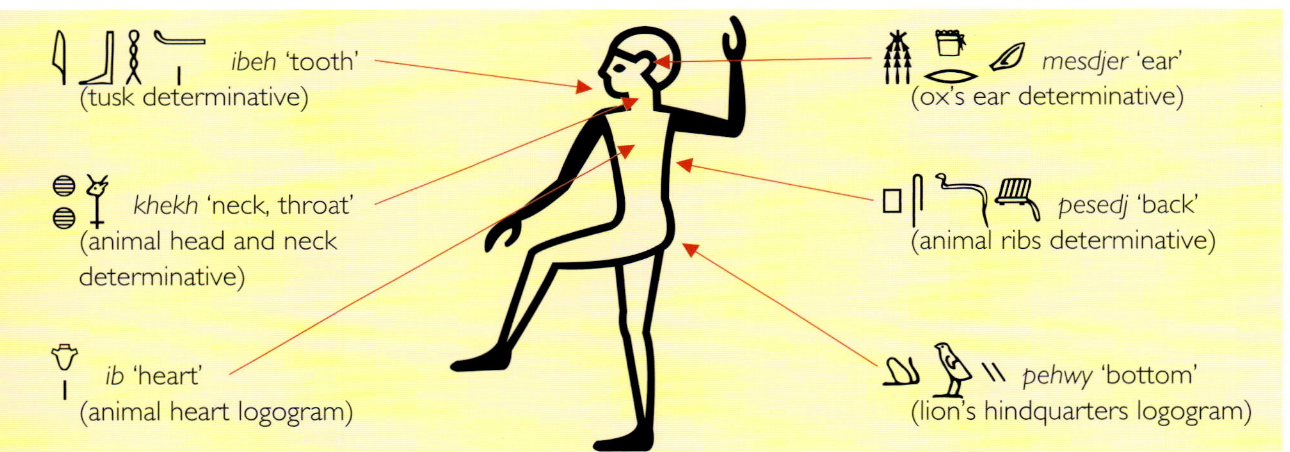

Pets' Names

Throughout Egyptian history it was common for the pets of noblemen and women to be depicted trotting at their heels as they performed their duties, or sitting by their feet as they received offerings. In a few instances, the animal's name is recorded, which was a particular honour for the animal because it assured an eternal memorial. It is likely that all pet animals had names, but it tends only to be dogs' names that are captioned in tomb scenes. Cats are very often shown sitting under their owners' chairs, but their names are not usually given. There are exceptions: the cat of the nobleman Puyemre who lived in the New Kingdom is depicted sitting facing his chair with his name above him: *Nedjem* 'Sweetie'. We also know the name of the cat that belonged to the brother of the infamous 'heretic' king Akhenaten in the New Kingdom: named *Ta-miut* '*The* Cat', this royal pet was provided with her own stone sarcophagus inscribed with funerary prayers usually reserved for people.

Dogs could be named for a certain quality they possessed, such as their colour: (e.g. *Hebny* 'Ebony'), but often their names reflect their relationship with their owner. Two dogs in the Old Kingdom were named *Seneb-neb-ef* 'The well-being of his master'. The nobleman Senbi's dog was named *Tjau-en-ankh-en-Senbi* which means 'Senbi's breath of life'.

Sekhemka, an official who lived in Dynasty 5, called his dog *Pesesh* 'the one who shares' ('Partner') and had him depicted twice in his tomb sitting under his chair:

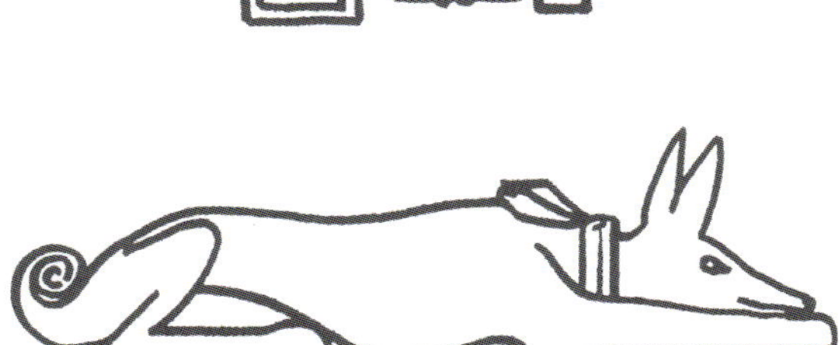

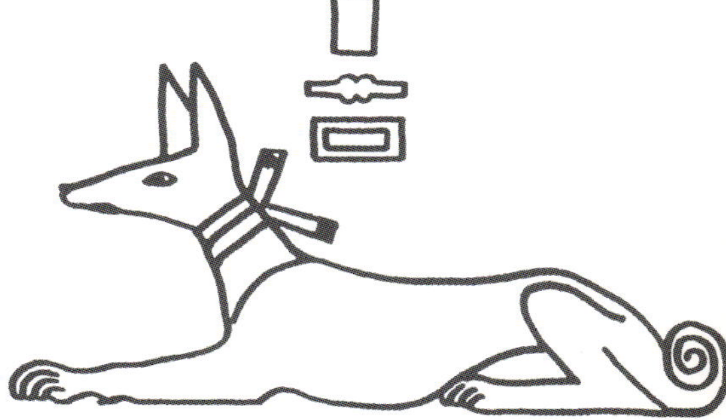

Pesesh is shown in two different positions – sleepy with his head on his paws, and wide awake with his nose in the air. In each case, the hieroglyphs that write his name are arranged to match his pose.

Some dogs have rather enigmatic names which can be read in different ways: for example, *Hemu-ma* the dog belonging to a nobleman in the Early Middle Kingdom. *hemu* means 'steering oar', and *ma* means 'lion', so the dog's name may have been 'Steerer of lion(s)'. It has been argued, however, that *hemu* might be a humorous way of describing an animal's tail (literally, its rudder), and so the dog's name might mean 'Lion's tail'. Dogs are often depicted accompanying their masters into the desert to hunt game, and so

Write Your Pets' Names in Hieroglyphs

Put your own pet's name into hieroglyphs (use the single-consonant signs on page 19 to spell out the sound of the name) and add a suitable determinative:

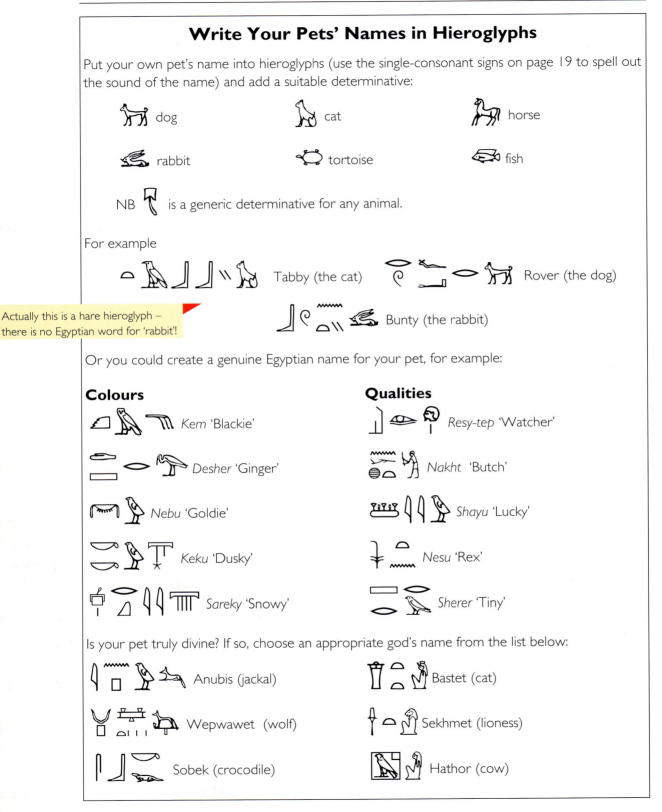

 dog  cat  horse

 rabbit  tortoise fish

NB  is a generic determinative for any animal.

For example

 Tabby (the cat)  Rover (the dog)

 Bunty (the rabbit)

Actually this is a hare hieroglyph – there is no Egyptian word for 'rabbit'!

Or you could create a genuine Egyptian name for your pet, for example:

Colours

 *Kem* 'Blackie'

 *Desher* 'Ginger'

 *Nebu* 'Goldie'

 *Keku* 'Dusky'

 *Sareky* 'Snowy'

Qualities

 *Resy-tep* 'Watcher'

 *Nakht* 'Butch'

 *Shayu* 'Lucky'

 *Nesu* 'Rex'

 *Sherer* 'Tiny'

Is your pet truly divine? If so, choose an appropriate god's name from the list below:

 Anubis (jackal)

Wepwawet (wolf)

 Sobek (crocodile)

 Bastet (cat)

 Sekhmet (lioness)

 Hathor (cow)

their names often reflect their ability to marshall animals, e.g. *Meniu-pu* 'He is a shepherd'.

Most owners clearly adored their dogs. One man's pet was called *Tep-nefer* 'Perfect Specimen'! However, it seems that the feeling was not always mutual: one Theban official called his dog *En-mereni* 'I don't like (anyone)' (pictured right).

So just like those of humans, dogs' names can tell us a lot about what they were like. It seems likely that *Aay* 'Donkey' was stubborn, and that *Degem* 'Gloomy' was rarely in a good mood.

En-mereni ('I don't like anyone') under his master's chair. Middle Kingdom.

Animal Symbolism

In hieroglyphs, animal signs in particular were put to a special use. Words in Egyptian were usually given a determinative (meaning sign) which meant that they had to be summed up with some kind of image. With many words, this was easy; for example, the word for 'elephant' could have a specific elephant determinative , or the more general animal sign, . But certain words were not easily visualized. How do you picture 'love' or 'greed'? The Egyptians had a solution to this problem – animal determinatives. The cow suckling her calf was the perfect symbol of motherly affection, and so this sign stands as the determinative for the verb *ames* 'to feel affection'. The crocodile sign acts as the determinative of ten words describing aggression, greed and power:

The painting of this dog, with his name *Ankhu* 'The Lively One' written above him, comes from the tomb of Djehutyhotep. Middle Kingdom.

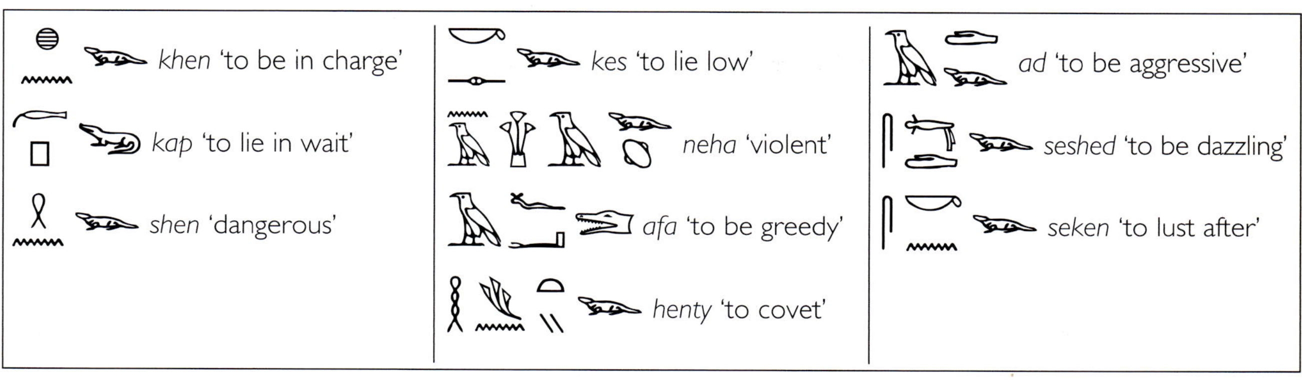

khen 'to be in charge'	*kes* 'to lie low'	*ad* 'to be aggressive'
kap 'to lie in wait'	*neha* 'violent'	*seshed* 'to be dazzling'
shen 'dangerous'	*afa* 'to be greedy'	*seken* 'to lust after'
	henty 'to covet'	

The most common animal determinative used in this special way is the sparrow. Egyptologists call it 'the bad bird' because it is used to determine over 500 words connected with evil, pain, misery and disaster. Originally the sign was only used in the word *nedjes* 'small', but it quickly expanded its range of meanings and came to represent a smallness in other things:

health: *men* 'to be ill'

wealth: *iad* 'poor'

happiness: *ahmet* 'sorrow'

wits: *wekha* 'idiot'

memory: *mehy* 'to be forgetful'.

Ironically, we are not sure what the Egyptian name for a sparrow was. It certainly seems to have been a bird of bad omen.

Drawing of the mythical animal sacred to the god Seth.

One of the most widely used animal determinatives alongside the bad bird is also one of the most complex to explain. The identity of the so-called Seth animal (left) has puzzled both Egyptologists and zoologists for over 150 years. It has the body-shape of a dog, which gives it a muscular physique and clawed paws, and a curved snout. It usually has some sort of weapon for a tail, most commonly an arrow but sometimes a club or a forked stick. The Seth animal has been jigsawed together quite deliberately from different components to be an enigma, and one that bristles with aggression from the tips of its ears to its tail. It is named *sha* 'the desert dweller' after the region that the Egyptians considered to be the end of the civilized world. The Seth animal sign was therefore the perfect determinative for words describing anything strange or disruptive to the natural order of the world, such as storms and malevolent weather:

neshny 'storm'

keri 'thunder'

It is also used in words describing violent noise and activity in the human and animal spheres.

seha 'chaos'

keheb 'to disturb'

hemhem 'to roar'

It may also be used as a determinative of words for illnesses, which the Egyptians classified as disruptions of the body's normal state of health. In usch cases, the sign takes the form of the god Seth rather than the Seth animal:

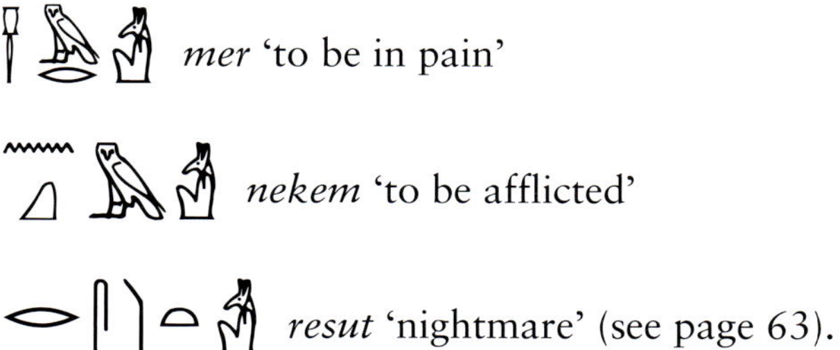

mer 'to be in pain'

nekem 'to be afflicted'

resut 'nightmare' (see page 63).

5 Practical Hieroglyphs – Words and Phrases in Egyptian

The ancient Egyptian language is incredibly rich in self-explanation. In putting the elements of their world into words, the Egyptians left behind such strong imprints of their patterns of thought that we can almost see through their eyes. Many things for which we have just one word were described by the Egyptians in vivid phrases. This chapter concentrates on those words and phrases, and as such is a guide to various aspects of the Egyptians' experience of the world in their own words.

The Body and Bodily Experiences

Word and vocalization	Meaning	Literal meaning
ra ib	'the stomach'	'the mouth of the heart'
mut remetju	'womb'	'the mother of people'
medet ib	'heartbeat'	'the voice of the heart'
khem djet	'to faint'	'to not know your body'
sekem nes	'wise'	'grey-haired of tongue'
au deret	'generous'	'outstretched of hand'
khenu awy	'an embrace'	'(being) within two arms'

The Physical World

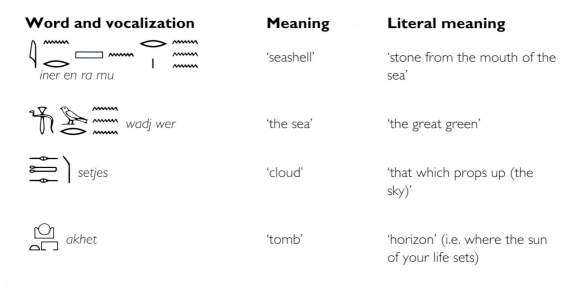

Word and vocalization	Meaning	Literal meaning
iner en ra mu	'seashell'	'stone from the mouth of the sea'
wadj wer	'the sea'	'the great green'
setjes	'cloud'	'that which props up (the sky)'
akhet	'tomb'	'horizon' (i.e. where the sun of your life sets)

The Emotional World

The Egyptians believed that every thought and feeling originated in the heart. This is why it was the heart of a person that was weighed against the Feather of Justice in the Hall of Judgement in the Afterlife to determine his or her moral worth. Emotions were considered to be physical events that the heart experienced and soaked up during life. After death, however, the heart developed a dangerous independence, and the Egyptians actually composed spells to make sure that it did not betray their darkest secrets. All of the words for various feelings below are described as physical conditions of the heart:

The scribe Ani worshipping his heart. New Kingdom.

States of Being

Word and vocalization	Meaning	Literal meaning
au ib	'happy'	'broad of heart'
as ib	'impatient'	'quick of heart'
wemet ib	'stout-hearted'	'thick of heart'
wer ib	'insolent'	'great of heart'
weha ib	'capable'	'released of heart'
senek ib	'haughty'	'greedy of heart'
kefa ib	'trusty'	'uncovered of heart'

Actions

Word and vocalization	Meaning	Literal meaning
am ib	'to be neglectful'	'to swallow the heart'
ia ib	'to vent anger'	'to wash the heart'
pak ib	'to long for'	'to be thin of heart'
pedj ib	'to be glad'	'to stretch out the heart'
redi ib em-sa	'to worry about (someone / something)	'to send the heart after (someone /something)'

her ib kemi sepet	'charming and discreet'	'pleasant of heart, gummed of lip'
senaa ib	'to soothe'	'to make the heart smooth'

Phrases

Word and vocalization	**Meaning**	**Literal meaning**
imy ib	'favourite'	'one who is in the heart'
en set ib	'darling'	'of the place of the heart'
hery ib	'the one within the heart'	'a middle child'
sewedja ib	'a letter'	'that which soothes the heart'

Shades of Meaning – Words and their Determinatives

The examples above show that what we tend to translate as a single word in English can be broken down into individual components in Egyptian to reveal deeper meanings. The same thing can be done with single words in Egyptian, because they too can be broken down into components: their phonetic stem (sound signs) and one or more determinatives (meaning signs). Words in Egyptian can express rich meaning because they combine both sound and meaning signs, and especially because those meaning signs can be altered to suit the context.

seti 'to shoot' is made up of a phonetic stem (the hieroglyphs shown in black in the box below: *s* + *t*) and two determinatives (shown in red in the box below): the first shows the hide of an animal pierced by an arrow – a specific representation of the result of shooting something and so a visual representation of the action of the word. The second determinative shows a man wielding a stick, the usual determinative of any kind of action involving force. Simply by changing the determinatives, or adding to them, many different nuances can be teased out of the stem, *seti*, with its basic meaning 'to shoot'; below are just a few examples:

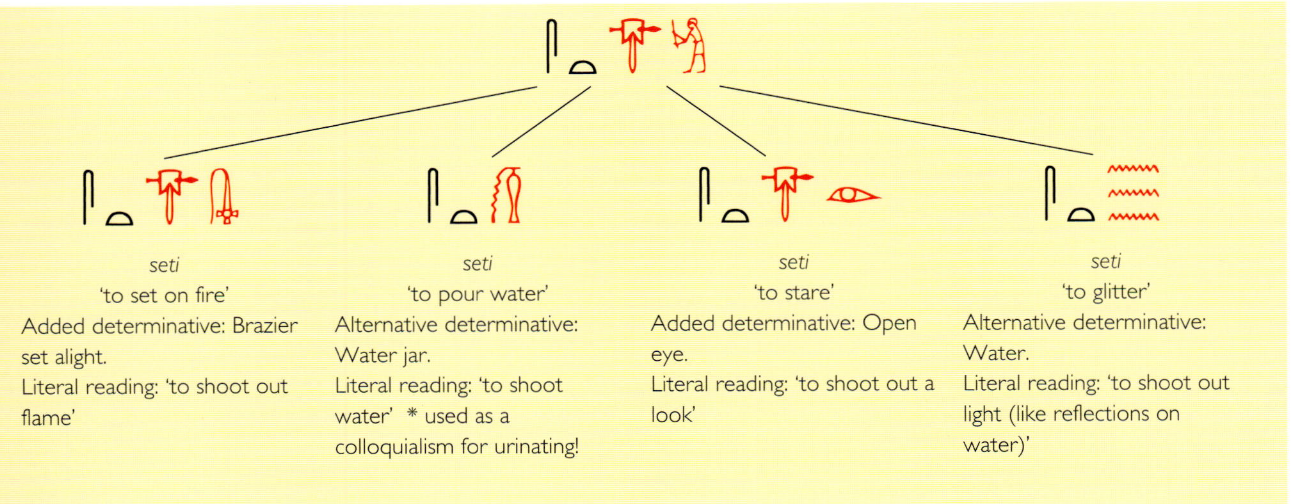

seti
'to set on fire'
Added determinative: Brazier set alight.
Literal reading: 'to shoot out flame'
seti
'to pour water'
Alternative determinative: Water jar.
Literal reading: 'to shoot water' * used as a colloquialism for urinating!
seti
'to stare'
Added determinative: Open eye.
Literal reading: 'to shoot out a look'
seti
'to glitter'
Alternative determinative: Water.
Literal reading: 'to shoot out light (like reflections on water)'

A great deal of metaphor is involved in the ways in which these words get their meaning. Yet, it is quite possible that all of them sounded alike when they were spoken out loud – remember, determinatives are not pronounced. When speaking, the Egyptians must have relied on context to hone the nuances of each appropriately, just as we do when we use words like 'reed' and 'read'. But in writing, each altered determinative adds something to its word, especially in the last case of *seti* 'to glitter'. There are too many similar examples to list, but here are a few particularly poetic pairings of words and determinatives:

The phonetic stem literally means 'bright thing'.

seshed 'window'

Determinatives: the house sign represents the larger whole of which a window is a part. The lidded eye refers to something that can open and close, and through which you see.

The combined effect of phonetic stem and determinative describes a window as 'the bright eye of the house'.

The phonetic stem means 'drunk'.

tekh 'drunkenness'

Determinatives: the foreign land sign as well as the usual beer jar.

Combined effect: drunkenness is envisaged as a faraway place. This writing is from a poem describing the bliss of death as like 'sitting on the edge of (the land of) drunkenness'.

The phonetic stem literally means 'that which keeps you awake'

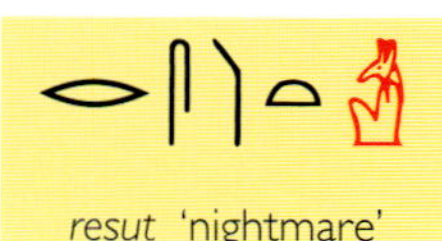

resut 'nightmare'

Determinative: the god of chaos, violence and illness, Seth.

Combined effect: a nightmare is 'a violent awakening'. This word is only attested in one text! Usually *resut* has an eye determinative and just means 'dream'.

The basis of the phonetic stem is the verb *weni* 'to hurry'. The doubling of the *wen* sound gives the idea of a repeated movement.

wenwen 'to sway back and forth'

Determinative: a lock of hair provides a typical example of something that sways.

Combined effect: this word is actually used of the swaying of a child in its mother's womb. The lock of hair determinative conveys the gentleness of the motion.

The phonetic stem *kap* means 'to be hidden' so the literal reading is 'that which is hidden'.

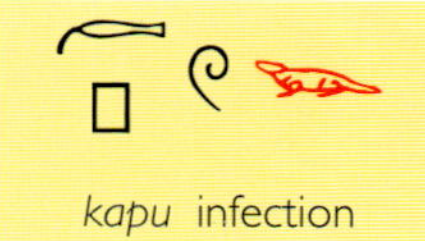

kapu infection

Determinative: crocodile, which is often used as a symbol of greed, aggression, danger, and so on.

Combined effect: this word is used once in a medical text to describe an infection lurking below the surface of the patient's skin like a crocodile beneath the water.

Passage from the Book of the Dead on the coffin of Pasenhor.

ser 'one who prophesies' has a giraffe determinative, which defines prophesying as the ability to see what is coming from a distance!

Write Your Own Egyptian Greetings

Many letters survive from ancient Egypt, both real correspondence and what are called 'model letters' which apprentice scribes wrote out for practice. From these and other texts we can gather a variety of greetings, well-wishes and insults.

Greetings and goodbyes

iy 'Hey!'

inedj her-ek – 'Hello!'

ir-ek heru nefer – 'Have a good day!'

nefer seneb-ek – 'Farewell!'

ikh rekh-ek su – 'Take note of it; N.B.'

huiu imi en-ef meret – Alas, you've got to love him!

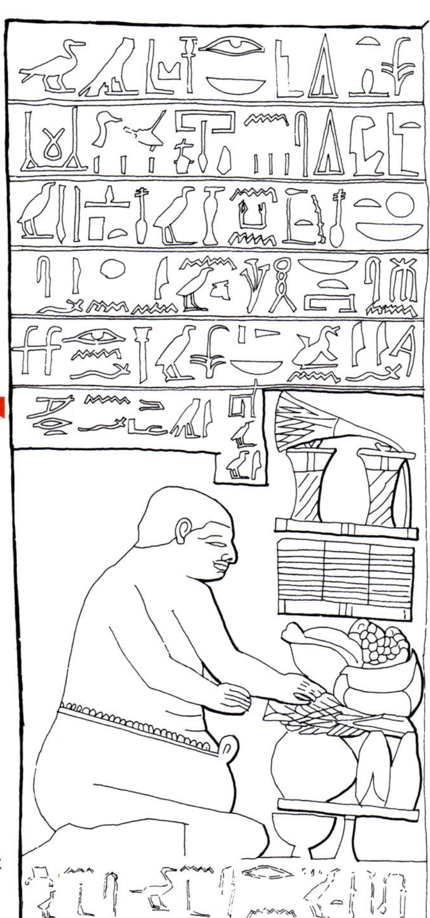

Stela of a chubby harpist named Neferhotep which starts with conventional offering prayers, but finishes rather unconventionally. Middle Kingdom.

imi ib-ek – 'Pay attention!'

em dyt haty-ek em-sa-i – 'Don't worry about me!'

wedja ib-ek – 'Cheer up!'

seneb-ti er per-ek – 'Bon voyage!'

Well wishes

ankh! wedja! seneb! – Life! Prosperity! Health!

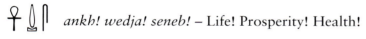

demi en-ek reshut tjeheh – 'May joy and delight cling to you!'

kab-ek renput neferu – 'May you multiply happy years!'

iu-ek men-ti mi na wenut – 'May you be established like the hours!'

peteri-ek nefer sedjem-ek nedjem – 'May you see well and hear happily!'

imi renpy-ek – 'May you feel young again!'

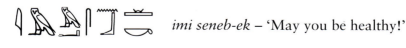

imi seneb-ek – 'May you be healthy!'

Well wishes can be abbreviated:

ankh-ek
May you live!

wedja-ek
May you be healthy!

seneb-ek
May you flourish!

user-ek
May you be powerful!

nakht-ek
May you be strong!

imi ankh-ek – 'May you live!'

seta-tu en-ek teka em gereh er webenet shu her shenbet-ek 'May a torch be lit for you in darkness until the sun shines on your breast!'

Harsh words

The Egyptians were not always polite with each other. Stories, letters and even scenes from tombs include many harsh words. Each of the insults below is real.

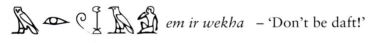

wekha khem khet penek mu – 'Fool! Idiot! Spouter of Water!'

em ir iker khenmes – 'Don't be smart, mate!'

em ir wekha – 'Don't be daft!'

pa adjed binwy depet – 'You foul-mouthed pipsqueak!'

sewered pu djed en-ek – 'Just talking to you is exhausting!'

pety iref pa ib – 'What's with this attitude?'

ib-ek teftef haty-ek mehy – 'Your heart is disturbed and your senses scattered!'

ger-ek akh set er teftef-ek – 'Your silence is better than your blethering!'

aka nes-ek! – 'Straighten your tongue!'

iry-ek en-ek khenemsu em-sa na weneshu – 'You're acting like a mosquito after wolves!'

bin-tu er semen en wedjebu pa ashau gau 'You're worse than the Nile goose of the river-bank that abounds in mischief!'

iry-ek en-ek ruyet em ta at en na atekhu 'You've made a home for yourself in the brewery!'

hetepu neferu en ka-ek! en iu mitet!
'Lovely offerings for your soul – there's been nothing like it!'

A sarcastic foreman prepares to punish two tax defaulters with blows. His taunt is bitter – if they've been hoarding supplies to feed their souls in the Afterlife, they're in for something else in the meantime. From the tomb of Khentika. Old Kingdom.

Roman Period graffito from the Temple of Philae of the name B. Mure. Underneath someone has added in Latin *stultus est* 'is stupid!'

mek-tu mi depet nen sekhery 'You're like a boat without a captain!'

haty-ek em mi kha! – 'Your mind's like an empty room!'

Laments

When they felt like it, the Egyptians really knew how to complain. For example:

haty-i nen su em khet-i – 'My heart's not in my body,

iret-i bedesh em nu – my eye is faint through looking,

medu pena – (my) words are upside down.'

wedenu pu – 'That's heavy!'

tjau! tjau! – 'Have mercy!'

And finally – How Egyptian texts traditionally end:

iu-ef pu hat-ef pehwy-fy It has come from beginning to end.

In Conclusion

> Your love is more precious to me than soothing oil on weary limbs,
> it feels like the finest linen robes laid on the bodies of the gods...
> it tastes like date juice mingled with beer...
> My love, until the day of rest from weariness comes, I shall be with you every day...
>
> Fragments of a Love Poem on an Earthenware Vessel from Deir el-Medina

The Egyptians were very careful about what they bequeathed to eternity. The images presented to us in tombs and temples of Egyptian life are therefore very much idealized, for the Egyptians were determined to preserve only the best of themselves. So when kings emblazoned temple walls with texts detailing their great campaigns, or when a nobleman carved a stela with the story of his life, the emphasis was on the ideal. Kings never faltered, noblemen were always strong and good, the women in their lives stayed young and beautiful.

In less formal texts we start to see that careful guard slipping. Old friends toss sarcastic remarks at each other in letters. Gods and kings behave like ordinary people in literary tales and embarrass themselves. In poems like the one above – sketched languidly in ink on a drinking vessel perhaps filled once with sweet wine and intended as a token of love – lovers pour their feelings out to one another. If we are looking for glimpses of ordinary Egyptian life, these tend to be the places we explore.

But deeper within the language these texts use, in the tiny details of the hieroglyphic script itself, even more vivid snatches of reality shine through. By exploring the seemingly innocent array of names the Egyptians gave themselves and the elements of their world and especially how these names were put together, we can see that alongside the sobriety and superstition which we perhaps expect of the Egyptians, there was also much humour and vivacity in their lives. Using hieroglyphs taught them to capture even the most complex and abstract forces in images – perhaps that is why they write such expressive love poems and why, in turn, their words explain the people who used them so well.

It has been the aim of this book to let you see the world of the ancient Egyptians as they saw it and to give you the ability to use their words for your own writing. The Egyptians enjoyed pouring as much meaning as they could into their words and had a lot of fun using hieroglyphs – I hope you will too. If you are interested in learning more about the ancient Egyptian language, or about Egyptian life in general, there are suggestions for further reading on pages 78–80.

Shemes ib-ek – Pursue your desires!

How to Draw Your Own Hieroglyphs – Some Hints and Tips

Some hieroglyphs are basic shapes and are easy to copy: like 𓐍 or 𓈖 . Birds, animals and people are trickier, but there are ways to simplify signs to make them easier to draw. Try following the steps below:

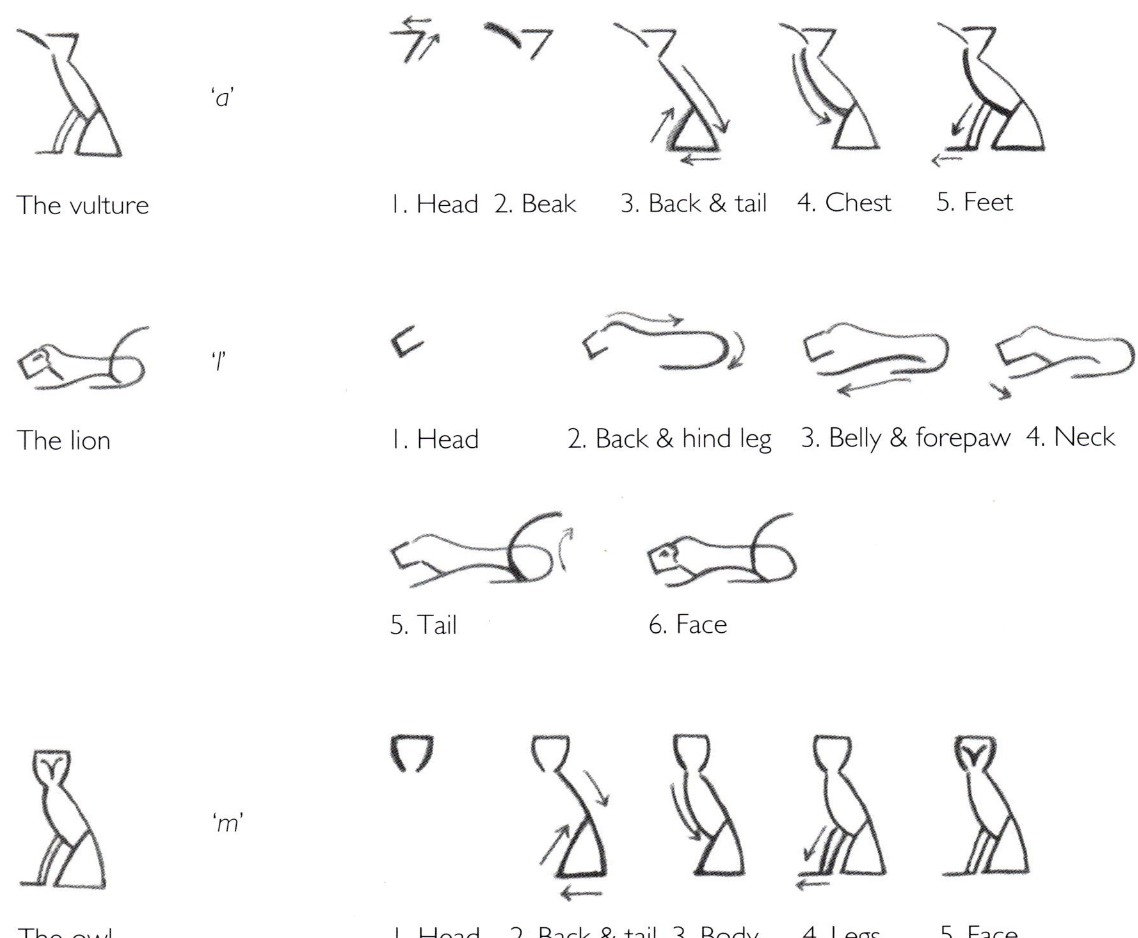

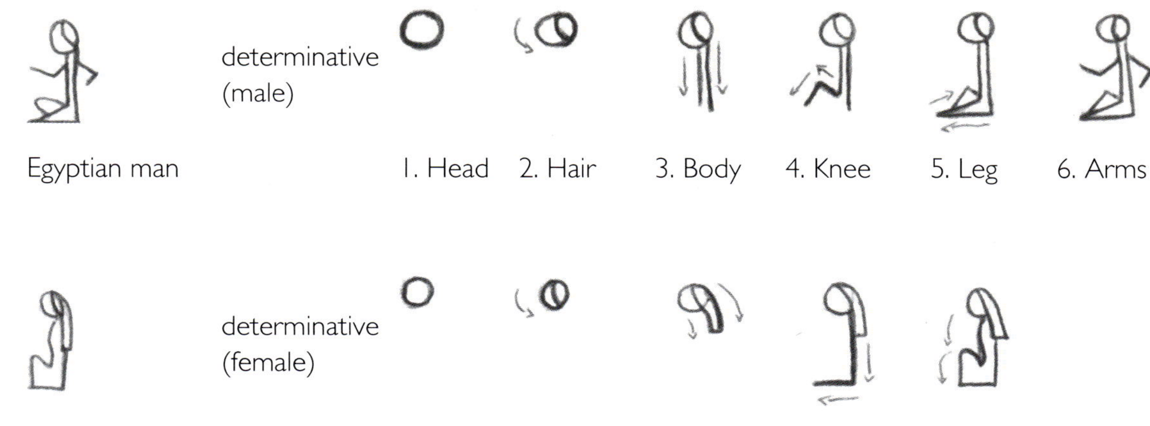

determinative (male)
Egyptian man
1. Head
2. Hair
3. Body
4. Knee
5. Leg
6. Arms
determinative (female)
Egyptian woman
1. Head
2. Face
3. Long Hair
4. Back & leg
5. Chest & knee

Translation and Transliteration

When translating Egyptian texts, most Egyptologists will first 'transliterate' the hieroglyphs into sound values using a special set of characters. Some of these characters are simply alphabetic signs (e.g. *d*, *t*, *f*), whereas others convey sounds that are not present in English (*ḳ*, *ṯ*, *ꜣ*). The table below lists the transliteration characters for all the one-consonant signs in the order that Egyptological dictionaries usually use.

Inevitably, some information is lost in the transliteration stage. Determinatives are not usually included in transliteration, even although they often differentiate words or add to a word's meaning. It is also impossible to convey orderings of signs to take note of any graphic or honorific transposition. Despite these limitations, transliteration provides a 'shorthand' way of noting down the content of texts without having to draw the hieroglyphs out.

Transliteration of one consonant signs

(with conventional pronunciations)

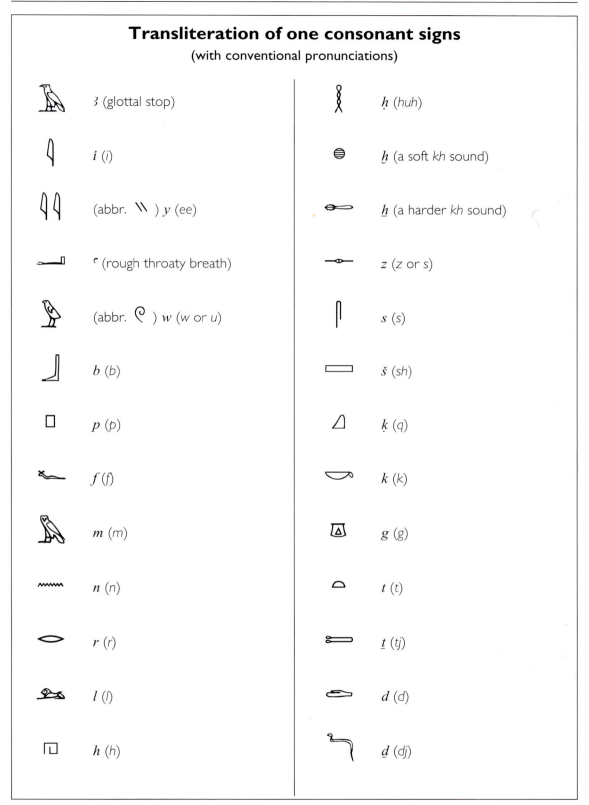

ꜣ (glottal stop)

ỉ (*i*)

(abbr. \\ ) *y* (ee)

ꜥ (rough throaty breath)

(abbr.) *w* (*w* or *u*)

b (*b*)

p (*p*)

f (*f*)

m (*m*)

n (*n*)

r (*r*)

l (*l*)

h (*h*)

ḥ (*huh*)

ḫ (a soft *kh* sound)

ẖ (a harder *kh* sound)

z (*z* or *s*)

s (*s*)

š (*sh*)

ḳ (*q*)

k (*k*)

g (*g*)

t (*t*)

ṯ (*tj*)

d (*d*)

ḏ (*dj*)

Glossary

Anthropomorphic	'Human' form; in human shape.
Coffin Texts	Collection of funerary spells to help the deceased in the Afterlife. Used mainly during the Middle Kingdom; derived from the Pyramid Texts.
Cosmogony	Creation myth.
Determinative	Hieroglyphic meaning sign with no sound value used only in writing to sum up a word or to supplement its meaning.
Dynasty	Succession line of kings, usually related.
Early Dynastic Period	Dynasties 0–3 (*c*.3100–2600 BC).
Faience	Bluish-green man-made material popular for amulets and decorative items.
First Intermediate Period	Dynasties 7–11; period of political instability (*c*.2150–1950 BC).
Graphic transposition	Placing of a sign or signs out of the expected grammatical order for aesthetic reasons.
Greco-Roman Period	Final phase of Egyptian history under the Ptolemies and Roman Emperors (332 BC – AD 395).
Ideogram	See logogram.
Inundation	Annual flooding of the River Nile; the silt deposits left when the water receded made agriculture possible in Egypt, which was otherwise a desert country.
Honorific transposition	Placing of the signs in the name of a king or a god out of expected grammatical order as a sign of respect.
Hyksos	Term used of the Asiatic kings who ruled Egypt during Dynasties 15–17.
Justified	Title given to those who passed the final test of morality in the Hall of Judgement and so could enter the Afterlife.
Lady of the House	Title of Egyptian noblewomen.

Late Period	Dynasties 25–30 (*c*.700–331 BC).
Logogram	Hieroglyphic sign with both sound and meaning; used to represent words directly with an image. Also known as 'ideogram'.
Middle Kingdom	Dynasties 12–14 (*c*.1950–1650 BC).
New Kingdom	Dynasties 18–20 (*c*.1550–1050 BC).
Obelisk	Tall column with pointed tip, commonly set up in front of temple gateways.
Old Kingdom	Dynasties 4–6 (*c*.2600–2150 BC)
Phonogram	Hieroglyphic sign used for its sound value only.
Pyramid Texts	Collection of funerary spells to help the deceased in the Afterlife. Used mainly in the Old Kingdom; exclusively for royalty at first.
Ramesside Period	Term for Dynasties 19 and 20 of the New Kingdom, when a number of kings had the name Ramses.
Scribal palette	Wooden tray for pigments and pens used by scribes.
Scribe	Someone who composed texts.
Second Intermediate Period	Dynasties 15–17; period of political instability and rule of the Hyksos kings (*c*.1650–1550 BC)
Sound complement(s)	One consonant phonogram used to 'echo' the final consonant(s) of a two- or three-consonant phonogram.
Stela	Monument erected to commemorate a person or event. Plural: stelae.
Third Intermediate Period	Dynasties 21–24; period of political instability (*c*.1050–700 BC).
Trilingual	Inscription in three languages, usually hieroglyphic Egyptian, demotic (cursive) Egyptian, and Greek.
Uraeus	Sacred cobra depicted rearing up in attack position.
Vizier	King's deputy; by the New Kingdom, there was a northern vizier based at Memphis and a southern vizier based at Thebes.

Further Reading

Grammars and Dictionaries

James P. Allen (2000)
Middle Egyptian. An Introduction to the Language and Culture of Hieroglyphs. Cambridge University Press, Cambridge.

Mark Collier and Bill Manley (1998; second edition: 2003)
How to Read Egyptian Hieroglyphs. British Museum Press, London.

Raymond O. Faulkner (1969)
A Concise Dictionary of Middle Egyptian. Griffith Institute Press, Oxford.

For Children

Richard Parkinson (2003)
Pocket Guide to Egyptian Hieroglyphs. British Museum Press, London.

On Decipherment

Richard Parkinson (1999)
Cracking Codes. The Rosetta Stone and Decipherment. British Museum Press, London.

On Hieroglyphs and Their Uses

Werner Forman and Stephen Quirke (1996)
Hieroglyphs and the Afterlife in Ancient Egypt. British Museum Press, London.

Richard H. Wilkinson (1992)
Reading Egyptian Art. A Hieroglyphic Guide to Ancient Egyptian Painting and Sculpture. Thames and Hudson, London.

Penelope Wilson (2003)
Sacred Signs. Hieroglyphs in Ancient Egypt. Oxford University Press, Oxford.

Collections of Egyptian Texts in Translation

Miriam Lichtheim (1973–1980)
Ancient Egyptian Literature. 3 volumes. University of California Press, Berkeley.

Andrea G. McDowell (1999)
Village Life in Ancient Egypt. Laundry Lists and Love Songs. Oxford University Press, Oxford.

Richard Parkinson (1997)
The Tale of Sinuhe and Other Ancient Egyptian Poems 1940–1640 BC. Clarendon Press, Oxford.

William K. Simpson et al. (third edition: 2003)
The Literature of Ancient Egypt: An Anthology of Stories, Instructions and Poetry. Yale University Press, New Haven.

General Guides to Egyptian History and Society

John Baines and Jaromir Malek (1980; second edition: 2000)
Cultural Atlas of Ancient Egypt. Checkmark Books, New York.

Patrick F. Houlihan (1996)
The Animal World of the Pharaohs. Thames and Hudson, London.

T. G. H. James (2005)
The British Museum Concise Introduction: Ancient Egypt. British Museum Press, London.

Stephen Quirke (1990)
Who Were the Pharaohs? A History of their Names with a List of their Cartouches. British Museum Press, London.

Ian Shaw and Paul Nicholson (1995)
The British Museum Dictionary of Ancient Egypt. British Museum Press, London.

Richard H. Wilkinson (2003)
The Complete Gods and Goddesses of Ancient Egypt. Thames and Hudson, London.

Toby Wilkinson (2005)
Dictionary of Ancient Egypt. Thames and Hudson, London.